Have You Met Miss Jones?

HAVE YOU MET MISS JONES?

The Life and Loves of Radio's
Most Controversial Diva

TARSHA JONES

 ONE WORLD | BALLANTINE BOOKS | *New York*

Published in the United States by One World Books, an imprint of The Random
House Publishing Group, a division of Random House, Inc., New York.

ONE WORLD is a registered trademark and the One World colophon is a trademark
of Random House, Inc.

ISBN 978-0-345-49748-2

Author photograph: Hot 97 and Devon Cass Photography

Printed in the United States of America

Designed by Stephanie Huntwork

Hate Me

love or hate me
it's always been that with me
hate my composure
hate that I am good at this
hate that my ratings are high

and love me for the same damn reasons

Miss Jones

CONTENTS

INTRODUCTION

From my earliest memory, nothing I did was ever right, so there came a time when I silenced myself and listened. Listened, and then believed everything the world told me about myself. I just shut the fuck up, and allowed people to treat me as if I had no value. No sense in arguing. They must be right. After all, most of them were older. And I loved them and depended on them to guide me in the ways of the world.

Every time I've tried to wear glass slippers, somebody has deliberately knocked them off of my feet. Because of that, I have walked the earth emotionally barefoot. And expressed my lack of self-esteem and rage in ways that clouded my judgment. I was a participant in a lot of drama. Didn't mean to be . . . it was never my intention.

The beat-downs came so often, I had to stop running and turn around and fight. Had to speak for myself. Had to fight for myself. Had to start swinging. And tell myself and the world that I have worth, I am valuable.

And though I still fight, there is a difference in my swagger. Instead of remaining silent . . . now I am talking. And I'm asking you:

Have You Met Miss Jones?

Have You Met Miss Jones?

ONE

BACK IN DA DAY

I almost killed my mother more times than I can remember. I didn't mean to. It just turned out that way.

Time after time, I watched her convulse, her body jerk, and her jaws flap like a hummingbird's wing, as she fell in and out of consciousness.

And I did nothing to help her.

"Get a spoon!" My stepdad, Sonny, would yell.

Chaos and radio static from the police and paramedics' walkie-talkies sounded throughout apartment 5G in the Astoria Projects, where we made our home. Uniformed men hovered over my mother's flailing body, attaching metal objects, trying to fix what I had done to her—again. My older sister Marcia screamed, "Momma is having a stroke!" My eldest sister, Audrey, ordered, "Get back in your bed! And don't move!" before disappearing into our parents' bedroom.

I sat on the edge of the twin bed with my spine reaching toward the ceiling. Alone. I was scared that my momma was really going to die this time, 'cause my dolls and games had been all over the floor when she called me for dinner. And she flipped. Sitting at the dinner table, my father scolded, "I done told you to stop aggravating your mother."

But I didn't listen. I got a hard head.

I didn't want to hasten her death by disobeying Audrey. Different, louder voices now reassured one another that my mother had stabilized. Cheating fate, I tiptoed toward my parents' bedroom, just as my mother groaned softly.

"Momma," I whispered to her. The uniformed adults ignored me—a nine-year-old little girl. My mother looked like a fragile china doll. "Momma, it's me, Tarsha," I said, gulping back tears. She didn't recognize anyone, as her gaze darted to each strange face in the bedroom.

A paramedic advised my stepdad, "Keep talkin' to her. Tell her who you are." My mother responded with double takes to anyone who spoke. Then slowly, the glaze over her eyes changed from stoicism to embarrassment. My mother cried from shame. And I cried too, wiping my tears with the sleeve of the fuzzy pink sweater my stepdad had recently bought for me. That morning, my mother had proudly escorted me to the school bus as I wore my sweater. On payday, my stepdad always bought me new outfits. My favorite was a white rabbit jacket with a matching muff and brown boots. My two older sisters were jealous because they had to wear hand-me-downs. Sonny would take pictures with his old instant Polaroid camera, as I posed in front of the hallway door with the lead-filled chipped white paint.

My mother whimpered, "My tongue . . . I bit my tongue."

"It's okay, Mommy." Audrey and Marcia tried to console her.

While the paramedics and the police gathered their equipment I reminded myself: *I better not do anything bad. Bring home good grades. Do all of my chores without being asked. Or my mommy might die. And it'll be my fault.*

My stepdad told me, "You aggravate her, that's why she has the seizures."

I was a bad little girl. I did bad things. I knew this because my step-dad repeatedly told me. And my bad things were sure to make my mother, whom I loved more than anything, leave me alone in this world. Alone because soon Audrey, at eighteen, was leaving for a place called college, and Marcia, who was nine months younger than Audrey, was wrapped up in following behind her. And Sonny, as I grew older, just became wrapped up in whatever. Whatever it was, it did not include me.

When my mother's seizures first happened, no one knew what to do about it. Later, she would be diagnosed with epilepsy.

My mother, Alyce Scott Jones, was the love of Sonny Tharpe's life. They met when she was twenty-four years old with two little girls and pregnant with me by my biological father, Billy Leon Jones. My mom had graduated number one in her high school class and was on her way to Spelman when she became pregnant with Audrey.

Even though Alyce didn't love Billy, they were forced by their parents to marry. My grandmother had gotten pregnant before she married and wanted to make sure that situation didn't happen with her only daughter.

Despite good intentions, Billy and Alyce were not prepared for the responsibilities of marriage and raising a family. Billy became involved with drugs and couldn't keep a job. My mom, being the bright woman she was, sized up the situation and divorced Billy.

Sonny and Alyce married after I was born. Sonny was Daddy. He gave me the Easters and Christmases that my sisters never got when they were my age.

"Goddamn it! Don't make me kill you!" my mother would scream. "I told you to stop!"

"Alyce, you better stop!" Sonny warned.

I would hear silence and then BOOM! BOOM! BOOM!

Friday evenings would always begin with laughter, but then alcohol would give way to harsh, violent words, which would merge with Marvin Gaye's "Let's Get It On" or whatever music my parents had been dancing to just an hour earlier. Even now, it's difficult for me to trust laughter, because I never know what emotion may follow. Apartment 5G was a place for my parents to unleash their internal demons that they couldn't show to the public. My home life hinged on the intersection of dysfunctional contradictions.

From the other side of my bedroom door, it always sounded like my mother would instigate physical fights with my stepdad. And then if he grabbed her wrists in an attempt to protect himself, and she got bruised, the fight would escalate. I didn't know what my stepfather had done, but my mother's threats would launch weekend-long beer-and-vodka-laced battles. The alcohol gave them both the courage to say things they would never utter sober.

Their fights frightened me. Rocking in my bed with a blanket over my head did not shield me from the tremendous fear that shook my body. No one called Alyce and Sonny's volatile relationship domestic violence back then. Our neighbors and family members sanctioned the violence with their silence. What you did in your house was your business. And you kept what family did to family behind closed doors. It was considered normal that Alyce used her fists on Sonny to relieve the depression she felt about her own life. Beneath her normally calm exterior, my mom was furious about her situation. She never expected her life to turn out the way that it did. And to wind up like the girls who hung out smoking in the bathroom, while she was the "good girl" who devoted herself to her studies in hopes of a better life, devastated her. This was not supposed to be her future—on welfare, with three kids, and a volatile relationship with her man. Sonny was a tortured man who retired after dinner to the bedroom to find a sense of peace before he returned to a daily life that heaped disrespect on him with low wages and long hours. Apartment 5G was the only place where his behavior didn't have any consequences.

Often my sisters and I were forced to take sides in their conflicts. If my stepdad spoke up for us and his doing so was the cause of the fight, my mother would stare at us and say, "This is all y'all fault. You think you getting away with this? I am not done with you." Or if we chuckled when my stepdad said something slick to her, she would later burst into our bedroom to punish us. Clicking on the lights, she'd wake us up by yelling, "Y'all think something is funny? Get out the fucking bed now and do some chores! We are gonna strip the paint right now!" our mother would scream with her hands on her hips.

"But it's midnight."

"You got energy to laugh, you got energy to pick up a fucking paintbrush!"

By Monday morning, everything returned to normal, as if nothing had happened.

During the good times, Sonny and Alyce would coo and laugh with each other. Wherever she was, he was. He took care of her every need and surprised her with gifts. Sonny drove her wherever she needed to go because my mother didn't have a driver's license. She worked when she was with my biological father, but she didn't work when she got with Sonny. As my mother's epilepsy became more frequent, she was afraid of having seizures in public places. My mother treated Sonny as if only he mattered. She didn't allow her women friends to distract or inject themselves in her marriage. When my stepdad would arrive home at three o'clock in the afternoon, weary from work, dinner was hot and ready. The television was on his channel, and the remote control was within his grasp. My mother, when she was feeling good, would hover around him, just in case he needed anything. Then with a full belly, he would retire to their bedroom to watch *The Flip Wilson Show* until he fell asleep. Their blissful routine would continue until the next weekend, when the cycle of drinking and fighting would begin again.

Everything I know about relationships, both good and bad, I learned from Alyce and Sonny; lessons that I am still trying to grapple with to this day. My mother taught me, without knowing it, that no matter how bad it got with a man, you never leave. Leaving is never an option. Appearances were important to my mother. It was important to maintain a united front. And that is part of the reason that I've had a hard time letting go of relationships even if they're abusive. Like a crack addict, I became intoxicated by tender moments, and when any kind of abuse occurred, I ignored it, still craving for just one more tender moment.

My babysitter overdosed on heroin. She was found on the back staircase of her floor in the projects. People stepped over her body and left her there for a while. Ignoring the dead body of my babysitter was not an act of cruelty. My neighbors stepped over a lot of heartache to get to the next point in their lives. For them, given a chance to avoid a painful situation was always the preferred strategy when they knew that a personal tragedy could await around the next corner.

The working poor who lived in the Astoria Projects watched and waited as life just happened. Another clique, made up of people who were either chronically unemployed or had dropped out of life, squeezed daily like grapes on the benches in front of the building. They made careers of being spectators to those who struggled to earn a living wage to feed their families.

Still, among the buildings in the Astoria Projects in Queens, New York, my building was considered the best, and for a while the cleanest. It was called the bus-stop building. Because it was the first building you saw when you got off the bus at the Projects' entrance. Everybody—especially the ones who sat in their windows all day—knew what time everybody else was coming and going.

"Hey, Tarsha! Where you going?" a nosy neighbor hanging out of the window would yell. "I'm going—" But before I could answer my mother would yell out of our window, "Tarsha! What did I tell you about yelling up at windows?!"

During the Christmas season, there was a floor decoration competition. Miss Eunice started the tradition. She decorated her apartment from the front door to the back bedroom with Christmas garland, tinsel, ornaments, streamers, and little clay Santa Clauses. Even the local drug dealers got caught up in the Christmas spirit and suspended their distribution of death until sundown, after everyone napped, satisfied from turkey dinners.

"Tarsha went home and told her parents that it was my fault that you all had to stay late after school," Ms. Tuohy, my second grade teacher, announced to my PS 17 classmates. I felt eyes boring into my back like a laser sharpshooter. My head hung low the rest of the day. The day before, Ms. Tuohy had kept us late after school, causing me to miss the school bus. My mother was never notified that I was going to be late. The white kids didn't have to take the bus, because their parents waited for them outside. There were no cell phones then, so my mother paced back and forth in front of our building. She hated being out of the apartment.

When I finally reached home, and after my mother stopped yelling, I told her why I was late. My mother phoned Ms. Tuohy and gave her a piece of her mind. So the next day, Ms. Tuohy retaliated when I got to school and embarrassed me in front of the entire class. I never told my parents what my teacher had done, because I was afraid the situation would escalate. Somehow, I knew that I would have to fight my battles on my own. That there would be no one to protect me. So I kept what I felt about what Ms. Tuohy had done to myself and decided to get anyone else who didn't like me to be my friend.

PS 17 was in an all-white school district, and I was the only black girl in the class. The white students never made me feel different, and the only time I felt black and like I didn't belong was when I got called on and I didn't know the answer to a question. But I was as smart, if not smarter, than most of my classmates. I was constantly being congratulated on the school intercom system for some achievement or other, such as reading one hundred books or making it to the National Spelling Bee.

My school friends lived in better neighborhoods and their parents liked me a lot. Invitations were always extended to visit them in their homes. Except on special occasions, I could never attend because of my mother's reluctance to leave the house and my stepdad's being too tired after working all day to drive me anywhere.

The first time I felt different from my white friends was during a game of Run, Catch, and Kiss. None of the white boys would chase after me. They would only run and chase my white girlfriends, who playfully screamed, "No, don't! No!" I beat up the white boys to stop them from kissing my white girlfriends.

Who wants to kiss me? Y'all can kiss me.

Finally I realized that the white boys didn't want to kiss me because I'm black. They didn't want to kiss a black girl, no matter how smart she was. At first I thought it was because I smelled different.

"Why does your coat smell like that? Is it the leather? Is it because it's a strange color?" For once, the questions from my classmates were not because they were trying to tease me. They were curious about that strange smell of my clothes. It was embarrassing when I realized that it was because of the smoke in the house. I hated that my parents smoked. And really hated when they told me to go to the store for a pack of Kool cigarettes.

But years later I would receive more attention than I could stand when I attended the mostly black Junior High PS 126. It seemed like the students' reason for living was to make my life miserable. They were determined to treat me like I was meant to be demeaned and attacked. Every encounter hinged upon or ended up in violence.

"What the fuck you say?" Kevin Foster yelled, spraying saliva within inches of my face. He was one of the boys who would squeeze my ass and breasts and then run away like a coward. Then they would tell other boys, "Tarsha easy, man!"

When I first started developing breasts and a butt, I felt really ashamed because badass boys would grab my body and encourage other boys to do it. I didn't fight back because I was afraid that I would get beaten up. There were never any witnesses, so this was yet another battle that I had to fight alone.

One day Kevin grabbed me and I had had enough and chased him down. He stopped and whirled up in my face, "What? What?" When I balled my fist and tried to block him from hitting me, Kevin punched me so hard that my thumb snapped out of joint. It remains dislocated to this day. Kevin was suspended from school. And after that fight, no one else attempted to violate me, because the word got back not to fuck with me or they'd wind up like Kevin.

My girlfriends who lived in the Projects and attended Junior High School 126 were very judgmental about me. I was very shapely, with a small waist and big butt, and my hair was long and thick. To them, there was always something wrong with the sneakers or jeans I wore or how my hair was styled. I would spend hours experimenting with different hairstyles, but my friends still always found something wrong with me. Their taunts and criticisms made me an introvert. I never wanted to attract attention to myself. "Sticks and stones may break my bones, but words can never hurt me" was the lie I always told myself. But the words did hurt, as I had not yet learned that I was valuable.

Looking back, I now see that they were just as insecure as I was. In a neighborhood where the adults consumed drugs and alcohol to dull their pain, these young girls desperately needed to overpower anyone they perceived as weak. And because I was a teacher's pet, I became the weakest link. I now know that one's self-esteem comes from within. Physically attacking another person only highlights the attacker's weakness.

TWO

WHEN I GROW UP!

Jonesy's Juice:

Karrine "Superhead" Steffans: When this chick ran crying from the studio because she didn't understand why the married men she'd called out in her tell-all book were upset, I knew she didn't have both oars in the water. Either that, or it was a perfectly choreographed plan so she could get her responses straight while she was on the hot seat. While husband/wife rappers Kool G Rap and Ma Barker screamed on her during the interview, I had the impression that she loved every single moment of the limelight. Even though she got pimped out and discarded, Superhead loves that she has exposed every man who thinks they got over on her. It's disgusting that she gets a kick out of inserting herself into the marriages of other people, and while she was getting off with half of hip-hop, she never took responsibility for her actions.

"**Y**ou got to be out your goddamn mind! There ain't no other woman!"

"Don't lie to me! Damn it! Don't lie to me! I wanna know the truth!"

Silence.

"All right! Goddamn it, what do you wanna know?"

"I wanna know the truth!"

Whispers.

Whatever Sonny said caused my mother to storm out of the house, slamming the door, with him tripping behind her, flailing his arms and questioning if she had lost her mind. I never bothered to follow them or peer out the window. As far as I was concerned, if you've seen one of their fights, you've seen them all. I blasted Denise Williams and Johnny Mathis's single "Too Much, Too Little, Too Late" on Audrey's record player, singing both Denise's and Johnny's parts. Audrey was gone so much that I was able to hog this wonder machine that would transport me away from the "Daily Fights at the Joneses'." Besides, I knew I would hear an instant replay of every stupid detail when my mother would blab to my great-aunt Nina on the telephone.

Aunt Nina was a dark-skinned woman with a colorful personality who lived in East Elmhurst, New York. Whenever my sisters and I got dressed up, it was usually because we were going to Aunt Nina's for the day. Everyone perceived her and her husband, Uncle Sam, as having achieved the American dream. But later it was revealed that they had hit the jackpot by stealing my mother's share of a lawsuit settlement from a car accident. My mother suffered painful back problems as a result of that accident, taking pain medicine on top of her pills for epilepsy.

Aunt Nina and Uncle Sam used the accident money to change their lives but were not concerned that Alyce, the niece they claimed they loved, was left scrambling for a financial and emotional life preserver, subsisting on public assistance. Uncle Sam and Aunt Nina stole all of it and purchased a beautiful home that was a suburban showcase.

Aunt Nina was a maternal presence to my mother and theirs was a relationship that my mother was not willing to discard no matter how the loss of the accident money affected her quality of life. The subject never came up and the relationship was cordial—that is, until both of them began drinking. The alcohol permitted them to speak what was in their hearts no matter how vulgar their words became. But they never separated angry at each other. Just before I would drift off to sleep, I would hear my mother say, "Okay, Auntie, talk to you tomorrow!" An hour before, they had been hurling nonsensical accusations, pouring from an open bottle of whatever was that evening's liquid pleasure.

At Junior High School 126 in Astoria, I was quiet until I was comfortable around my classmates, although I wasn't shy about raising my hand to answer questions, read out loud or write on the blackboard. "Pick me! Pick me!" was my constant cry in class. In seventh and eighth grade, it was crystal clear to my young eyes that the white kids had an advantage that my friends and I did not. Their parents were constantly involved, encouraging their kids, while my parents, though they did attend the parent-teacher conferences, only did so when there was a problem, not when I was excelling. Many of the parents of black kids couldn't find their way to the school to save their lives, especially on parent-teacher day. Teachers would sit twiddling their thumbs waiting for the parents of their students to arrive. Often the black parents would belittle the teacher if they had the nerve to flunk their child, even if the child hadn't been to school in weeks. In the eyes of some of the black parents, it was the duty of the school to raise their children, not vice versa. On the other hand, many of the white students seemed to be encouraged by their parents to excel. Their parents co-partnered with each teacher to make sure their children were properly educated. What I learned was that a child positively responds when the adults in their life have high expectations of them. Many of my black classmates suffered from low expectations by their parents.

"Tarsha is just not applying herself. She has potential, but she doesn't focus on her homework." Like a needle piercing my left temple, Sonny and Alyce coordinated squinting their evil eyes, to signal that there would be hell to pay as soon as we were out of earshot of school authorities. No matter how profane Alyce and Sonny could get in the seclusion of our apartment, when they met with my teachers, they were paragons of angelic parenthood. After assuring whatever teacher that my work or conduct would immediately improve, they would pelt me with a stream of rants all the way home. "Your sisters went there and if Audrey and Marcia could do it, you can do it. You stay in the goddamn house . . . hanging around them dumb-ass kids!"

While in my mind I rebelled, I would rarely talk back, especially if I was in close proximity to my mother's fist. If whatever I had to say came out louder than intended, I would pay the price with a slap upside my head.

When I didn't understand my homework, which was a lot of the time, I would daydream, and stare out of my bedroom window, watching kids in the neighborhood or the group of adults with too much time on their hands perch on the benches in front of the building. I tried to focus on my homework, but could not see the words on the page. Finally, I would toss the book on Audrey's former bed, which remained unused while she was away at college, and did what I liked to do: sing!

I would tiptoe over and click on Audrey's record player, with the volume real low. Diligently, I wrote down the lyrics to "I Want to Thank You" by Alicia Meyers and created my own magical stage as if I were on *Soul Train*. There were no videos then, so I had to create my own choreography. And the star was me! Singing gave me confidence and a sense of power, in that it was an activity I could do well, without question.

The television was left on with the volume blaring Eyewitness News' five-o'clock broadcast. And every single ceiling light and lamp in the apartment was on as if it were New Year's Eve and everyone had rushed to Flushing Meadows–Corona Park for the midnight fireworks. My book report for English class was done, so I used my mother's and stepfather's sudden absence to escape down the back stairs and pray that I would run into Eric, whom I loved madly, in my own twelve-year-old kind of way. Eric was a little older than me and didn't really know that I existed, which was fascinating. At home, I had grown accustomed to being ignored, so I equated his aloofness with affection. After I flaunted myself in front of him enough times, he began to interact with me without constantly looking around for his friends.

Like clockwork, Eric finished playing basketball around six o'clock every day, coinciding with my 6:00 P.M. curfew. Our "relationship" was quite simple really. I would see him. He would see me. I would talk to him. And he would talk to me. About stupid shit. Just when things were getting interesting, Sonny would sprint around the corner, wearing a stretched-out wife beater and wrinkled shorts, his ashy feet in flip-flops. Eric would always see my stepfather first. The terror scrawled across his face was my cue, and the dust Eric kicked up bouncing out of there was the other. "Get witchu later," I think Eric would mumble, rounding the corner farthest away from me, and holding his basketball like a pacifier under his brown-toned, lanky arm.

Daag. Busted.

The momentum in my "relationship" with Eric had been foiled again. After my two-week punishment for violating curfew, we—er, I—would have to start all over again. Eric was never interested enough to adjust his schedule to compliment mine.

No one explained anything to me about sex or menstruation. I got my period while my mother was in the hospital getting a hysterectomy. Marcia, who was home from college at the time, explained, "It's not a big deal. Hold on, I'll get you a pad." My friend Amanda taught me about boys. For some reason, she thought it was her life mission to dictate my sexual experiences. And I learned from her instruction: "You gotta kiss him" or "You gotta sex him." Amanda was also the first friend in my circle to get pregnant.

My mother paid more attention to my singing than I gave her credit for. Unbeknownst to me, she had heard me singing around the house. She knew that my talent really developed in the community center during the annual talent shows.

"What the hell is going on?" is what Audrey and Marcia's expressions read when they would arrive home from school. Once their eyes focused, they hollered laughing at the comical scene. My mother would make me dress up and perform songs from the musical *The Wiz,* wearing brown tweed gauchos that snapped in the front, a brown turtleneck and a matching hat. When Audrey and Marcia began mimicking me, I would run from the room in embarrassment. But my mother would call me back. "Let's go! You have to be dedicated."

Dedicated for what, I had no idea.

"Walk in time with the music, Tarsha . . . okay, now when the song goes 'put your left foot out' don't put your right foot out . . . okay, now pose with your hand behind your ear . . . that's it . . . again!"

I now wonder if I was a naive victim of Alyce's drunken stupor. I know I was her entertainment.

Sad, but funny.

"Nikki! Telephone! Come get the damn phone!" I took my time. I had been in the mirror pretending that I was Crystal Gale singing "Don't It Make My Brown Eyes Blue." So I didn't look like a complete ass, I removed the brown sweater from my head, which stood in for Gale's long brown hair. By the time I had dragged myself into the kitchen, my mother was slamming pots, having long since abandoned her Kool cigarette burning like cherry incense on the coffee table. Sonny was nowhere to be found. I picked up the phone receiver.

"Hello?" I said, sounding as nonchalant as possible.

"Whatchu doing, little gal?"

"Nothing." I didn't know what I was supposed to say.

"What do you mean, 'nothing'?"

"I dunno. Nothing. Just playing."

"Don't let me hear about you doing nothing!" And so it went. This was how my periodic telephone exchanges went with Billy, aka my biological father.

"Your father was very handsome," my mother would say, "but he never wanted to achieve his full potential." Billy wanted shortcuts in life. He wanted to be with cats on the street. And as a result, we ended up in the projects, and he back at home with his mother and adult siblings in Jersey City, New Jersey.

"All right, little gal, I love you madly. Put your momma back on the phone." Those were the words that I looked forward to hearing so I could return to my brown-sweater hair and Crystal Gale, or whoever I was pretending to be.

My mother would ask, "Why were you mean to your father?"

In reality, I wasn't trying to be mean; I was only following her instructions. And if I didn't have other plans, I obeyed adults, even if my intuition told me different. Plus, my mother always said that some adults would pick the brains of kids to try to find out what was going on in their house. My mother warned, "Don't you be telling people my house business." Sonny didn't appreciate Billy coming back on the scene. My stepfather considered Alyce, Audrey, Marcia, and me to be his family, biological or not. Legally married or not. Fighting all of the time or not. After all, Sonny had invested the time and sweat in raising and caring for another man's children. So he was afraid that with Billy's renewed attention, his own emotional investments would break his heart.

My sisters, Audrey and Marcia, remembered growing up with Billy until they were eight or nine. They had a clearer attachment to who their biological father was. When Sonny came along and tried to lay down the law, Audrey would say, "You're not my father! You can't tell me what to do." And yet there were moments when Sonny and Audrey bonded. They were both early risers. Sonny taught her how to separate sections of the newspaper so he could read them in the order he preferred, as they sipped hot coffee and ate breakfast together in a comfortable silence.

Nothing takes the place of being there.

"See, before I met Sonny I was married to Billy, your real father, and he wants to meet you. You are a very special little girl."

"Why?" I asked.

"Because most little girls don't have two daddies." Though that was a nice sentiment, my relationship with Sonny or Billy was never very deep. We never had a *Cosby Show* version of a father-daughter relationship. They asked a question. I gave an answer. Usually one word.

Billy asked. "Do you want to call me Daddy?"

"No."

"Pop?"

"No."

"Billy?"

"Yes."

Billy would take me to a diner every two weeks, and I could order whatever I wanted. I never asked him to explain his absence from my early life. In fact, it never occurred to me to do so.

The large two-family, two-story house he lived in became the drop-off point for me on the so-called father-daughter weekends. Billy would leave me playing with toys, while he ran the streets. His mother, my grandmother, didn't have much to say to me. "Nicole, wake up." "Here's your towel." "Nicole, your father told me to wake you up." "Here's your toothbrush." And neither did Uncle LC, who was wheelchair-bound and only grunted if you spoke with him. He used to be one of my dad's coolest brothers . . . a friendly, gregarious partier to the early hours. But his legs were amputated due to diabetes when he was about forty-eight years old.

It took me a while to realize that Billy was bribing me with shrimp cocktail, records, and toys so he could feel better about disappearing. Like clockwork, he would give me a menu to order from Blimpie.

And once he saw that I was set up with my sandwich, soda, and potato chips, he was gone, leaving me to eat alone.

Fortunately, my cousin Rhonda, who was a little older than me, lived upstairs. She had friendly girlfriends, money, and a driver's license. She started taking me places 'cause she thought I was cool. I would spend several weeks with her during the summer.

Though I never emotionally bonded with Billy, he ushered in my independence in the world beyond my Astoria neighborhood. He taught me how to travel from Astoria to Jersey City, through the maze of tunnels of 34th Street, the PATH train, and corridors to Journal Square buses. Boys, school, accomplishments, and questions were never discussed with Billy or Sonny, though. A male role model never answered the curiosities that I had about nearly everything in my life. And what I didn't figure out on my own just didn't get figured out.

"Remember what I told you. You don't say nothing . . . Just ball your fist up quietly at the side of your body . . . Keep your arm straight down . . . You focus on the part right between their eyes where you're going to punch . . ."

"Well, how do I know when to punch, Mom?"

"You'll know. 'Cause you feel it in your stomach. Don't waste your time talking back and wiggling your neck and alla that . . . But the minute the person is up in your face and you feel that they are about to swing . . . count to three and punch. Hit and bring it back. Hit and bring it back."

Those who can, do. And those who can't, teach.

Who knows where my mother learned to fight, because I never saw her hit on anyone except me, my sisters, and Sonny. Training sessions occurred after Andrea Barrett, a girl in my Glee Club, jumped on me. That's when my mother showed me how to protect myself. Tracy was one of those back-of-the-projects chicks that I was afraid of. Afraid because I knew the kind of building she grew up in . . . broken lightbulbs, dark hallways, and urine odors. She was light-complexioned with short hair and had a mean scowl. She wore big door-knocker earrings, mirroring older women she lived with. Some kids had a problem if you wanted to learn and make yourself into something. If you sat up straight, paid attention, and had the nerve to do your homework as best you could, you just might set yourself up for a beat-down. And if you had white friends, then some black kids hated you even more. Andrea Barrett and her ignorant-ass friends were just those types of kids.

"Shaddup, Tarsha!"

"No, you don't tell me what to do," I replied, wheeling around to face her. Next thing I knew, she had thrown me up against the piano. I remember thinking that she was smaller but stronger. She must have been used to fighting. Because fighting is what those people did in the back projects.

Everyone thought that I was a punk because I wasn't a fighter. And now, after getting my ass kicked, I was fair game for another beat-down.

When we weren't in school, Eric's sister Pam was very friendly toward me. Their mother liked me because she knew I wasn't one of these fast-tail girls. But when Pam was under Andrea's spell, she would go out of her way to roll her eyes.

Looking like Linda Blair in *The Exorcist*.

Now Pam had to prove herself. Prove that she was tough. And in her mind, I was just the patsy to add a notch on her belt.

Not.

One day in the hallway, in between classes, Pam ran up on the wrong me. The training I had undergone with my mother kicked in. I visualized the beat-downs that my sisters had put on both boys and girls, causing their parents to come ring our doorbell. Whatever Pam said, the next thing I knew, I had pummeled her in her eye. All of the frustrations, all of the backstabbing, all of the snickers, all of the name-calling, I took them out on her.

Pam and I were hauled off separately to the dean's office. Later, on the way home, Amanda ran over to me, excited. "Girl, you know you gave her a black eye." Now everybody wanted to walk home with me. I was Miss Popularity. Kids who had never even spoken to me were now grinning in my face.

"For real?" I asked.

"Yep, she gotta fucking black eye," Amanda said in wonder, her eyes bugging out of her head. Neither Alyce nor Sonny punished me, because they knew that those ratty-tat girls had been lying in wait to hurt me.

But today had been my damn turn.

Ten seconds. That's how long my first sexual encounter lasted. It was with Leon, aka Shamaine, who was a member of the Five Percenters, a black cult that grew in popularity in the 1980's with the philosophy that only black men could reach the highest level of perfection. He renamed me Queen Shaquanna, which I didn't let get back to my mother. Shamaine came from a good family but he made drug runs because he heard the streets louder than he heard his parents. Our rendezvous occurred in my living room, while my mother was in the kitchen looking for a fresh pack of cigarettes. At sixteen, Shamaine was a year older than me, and I should have known better. Before he came over, he smoked some weed and told me to wear a skirt. Shamaine also explained, "You can't get pregnant, because when a guy breaks a nut, what comes out is puppy water."

With all of his preplanning and scientific wisdom, nothing happened. And the nothing happened fast. The unrequited experience embarrassed us so much that we never tried or spoke about it again.

Early in my life, there seemed to be an unwritten rule that every boy who liked me had to have some crazy chick who wanted to fight me for his attention. When Eric finally paid me some attention, there was a bitch named Regina who bullied me by saying, "I'll fuck you up!" Regina tried every day to instigate a fight with me. She was outraged that I continued to ignore her ass. Later Regina found out that I had written Eric a letter while I was away at summer camp. When I returned home, Regina confronted me near the bus stop: "Don't be writin' him no more letters! Do you hear what I say?"

"Yeah, I heard you," I replied, as my head rotated, moving like a cobra. Ever since Regina began having sex with Eric, and I wasn't, she had lost her marbles. Admittedly, I was sexually naive. I wasn't sure how to interact with boys. And anything I did do was at Amanda's urging, or I just pretended to be confident in my skills. After Eric and I stopped messing around and Shamaine stepped back in, I believed that I had to have sex if I was going to keep a real boyfriend. I was tired of boys treating me like I was their little sister, and bitch-ass girls like I was their doormat. It would have been great if I felt I could have gone to Sonny or Billy for advice, but those were not the cards I was dealt.

I worked my long hair to my advantage, wearing it loose. I put water and grease in it so it could wave up. I washed and dried my jeans so they would fit tight, and wore Audrey's heels. After I left the apartment for school, I added lip gloss at Pam's house. I started hanging out with the fast girls in the back of the projects. And couldn't have cared less if Regina saw me.

Bitch, you're gonna just have to handle it now.

I was tired of being bullied. Just tired. And ready to get my sex game on.

During my first year of junior high school, the Glee Club saved my soul. That is where I met Ms. Patterson, a music teacher, who became the mentor that changed my life. Under her warm encouragement, my singing got noticed, because I was always asked to sing at graduations. Under the watchful eye of Ms. Patterson, I learned how to read sheet music and select song standards that were appropriate for my voice. Ms. Patterson wanted me to attend the prestigious High School of Music & Art—the school upon which the popular *Fame* movie and television program of the 1980's was based.

"I thank you, but I don't want Tarsha leaving this borough just to go to a school she could go to here."

"Ms. Jones, your daughter has tremendous potential to be a major talent in music. This is really an opportunity of a lifetime. And there are no schools of similar caliber in Queens."

At that point, I didn't have a spiritual relationship with God. Until Shamaine straightened me out, I thought God was a white man, with a white beard, who made sure we did good. Fair enough, God wasn't asking too much. I only prayed because some adult kind of threatened that it would be a good idea. No one ever saw me pray about something meaningful. I thought I looked corny. At dinner I would rush: "GodisGreatGodisGoodLetusthankhimforourfoodAMEN." But when no one was around at bedtime, I made the prayer personal to whatever dilemma I was going through. "Please, God, let Sonny lose weight and pass the physical." "Please let my father hit the number." Whenever I heard that somebody needed something, I prayed for it. The extent of the religious instruction coming from my mother was, "Make sure you say your prayers and thank God." And that was it.

"God? It's me, Tarsha. Can you make my mother change her mind so I can go to Music and Art? Thank you."

Eventually, my mother agreed.

The preparation for the audition for the High School of Music & Art was difficult but fun. Ms. Patterson worked with me on the sheet music. She helped me select songs that highlighted my voice, and ran skills with me. She talked to me about the possible opportunities there were in the world of music. For the first time ever, I was allowed to dream.

During the actual audition, I was extremely prepared. There was a tone test and a rhythm test. The hard part came in waiting to hear if I had passed the audition, though I felt confident. A few days later, during homeroom announcements over the school intercom, we heard: "May I have your attention? We are pleased to announce that Tarsha Nicole Jones has been accepted to the highly selective and widely acclaimed Fiorello H. La Guardia High School of Music & Art and Performing Arts in Manhattan."

I was leaving the Reginas, Tracys, and the Pams of the world behind.

Oh well.

THREE

MUSIC & ART

Jonesy's Juice:

Nas: Nas is one of the greatest rappers of our generation. I just wish that there weren't such long periods between each album. In every interview, Nas has dropped brilliance on hip-hop, culture, and politics, enlightening millions of listeners. Young and old can benefit from his teachings, especially those who don't read on the regular. When Nas puts it down on wax, he instructs a generation.

As the days of summer drew to a close, I became more thrilled about attending Music & Art. I was ready for new experiences and new friends. Sonny did two mock trips to show me how to get to Harlem alone on the crime-ridden bus and subway. One morning, a weird man kept bumping into me as if the packed A train forced him against me. I didn't realize until it was over that he had grabbed my crotch. I called him a bastard, but not menacing enough to intimidate him or to draw attention to the situation, because I felt ashamed. He stood there grinning as if I had complimented his haircut. Shaken, I left the train, and carried a heavy feeling at school the rest of the day.

Seeking sympathy, I reported the incident to Sonny that evening. He replied, "Your jeans are too tight," as if the molestation was my fault. He made me feel that I had brought it on myself, so I decided not to tell grown-ups anything and fight my own battles, letting the chips fall where they may.

The 125th Street subway platform was the transfer place for kids going to Music & Art. Groups of kids sung together and used their hands to improvise instruments. The majority of these kids were very talented, as opposed to the performers annoying people on the trains today. The other passengers never seemed to mind seeing happy and very loud kids.

My course load included the standard academics and also vocal music, arranging, senior chorus, gospel chorus, voice class, and music theory class. The creative environment at Music & Art helped me emerge from my shell. The comfortable, loudmouthed Tarsha showed up every day, and as a result I got my ass kicked in the process. Whoever said that girls are sugar and spice and everything nice is full of shit. They obviously didn't attend any of my schools. A bitch named Dorothy Lee posed as a friend to see what I was made of, but later picked a fight after school. She wanted to show everyone that if anyone was going to be the tough loudmouth freshman it was going to be her. After the crazy bitch beat me up, she apologized and wanted to be my friend.

At Music & Art, kids often socialized in segregated racial groups. The white kids were in one place and the black kids in another. Seems like the white kids got to hang for long hours after school. I had to get my black ass back to Queens, or there was going to be hell to tell the captain. It was the same routine every day, go home and do my homework, then do my chores, before hanging with my project friends. If it was dark or 6:00 p.m. by that time, then I wasn't allowed to go out at all. And there was no use trying to rush through my homework or my chores, lest I be summoned to return home and re-do what I had rushed through. The way I responded to my parents' rules, I of course was the most oppressed teenager in America. Surely, the Supreme Court needed to hear my case.

Many of my classmates went on to have stellar careers. Chastity Bono was either shy or just an antisocial classmate. Ricky Walters, later known as MC Slick Rick, was a sweet guy, but he hawked me like peanut butter on jelly and graduated at the end of my freshman year. Jennifer Aniston, the actress, who at that time was chubby, was a classmate. As we were waiting for the cafeteria doors to open, I asked her if John Aniston, who portrayed the character Victor Kiriakis on *Days of Our Lives,* was her father. "Omigod, how did you know?" she asked. She was shocked that I knew who her father was, unaware that my mother had been glued to *Days of Our Lives* for years. Tichina Arnold, who later starred in the television series *Martin* and *Everybody Hates Chris,* was my classmate and friend. Because she was always auditioning for paid gigs on television and movies, she infrequently attended school. But when comical Tichina was at school, she always had an entourage around her. And it was time to let loose and crack jokes in the back of the class. Some teachers gave up trying to tame her personality or talent. When she played Zena Brown from 1987–1989 on *Ryan's Hope,* I was amazed on our shopping sprees when she could drop big money without checking the price tag. Of course, I did more window than shopping.

"Well, Ms. Arnold, since you find everything so hilarious, why don't you give us something to laugh at. Stand up and sing *Gloria: Aria: Qui sedes ad dextram Patris . . .*" Ms. Ext thought that Tichina didn't know it, but she blew through it so effortlessly, it almost brought tears to your eyes. Everyone wanted to applaud, but we were afraid of Ms. Ext, so we just smiled at Tichina or slipped and gave her a low five. Not breaking her stride, Ms. Ext said, "Hmph, you think you are a star, don't you? Well, I've got news for you. You are just another student in this class. And you will never amount to anything!"

We still laugh about that to this day.

Still, Ms. Ext was my favorite and toughest teacher, because she gave a damn and pushed us to learn. She wanted us to be equipped to take on the world of music. I learned solfeggios, which are hand signals that correspond to each tone on the major and minor scale. She taught the inharmonic in between each note. I learned how to ascend the chromatic scale using sharps and descend using flats. This was very difficult to do. And if you didn't get it, she really embarrassed you.

Ms. Ext explained, "If you can master solfeggios, I guarantee that you will be advanced on the next level of instruction." I practiced all the way home and until I went to bed and all the way back to school the next morning. When Ms. Ext called on me, I aced that shit, while everyone else choked or never understood it in the first place. Totally out of character, Ms. Ext clapped and praised me. This was one of my proudest moments at Music & Art. I was a reluctant student in courses that I felt would have no impact on my ambitions to be a recording star. In my teenaged mind, a C average was good enough for me, and as long as I got 90s in my music classes, I couldn't have cared less about math and science. Alyce and Sonny held ongoing interrogations of me about my grades and continued to compare me to my sisters. In the meantime, Audrey and Marcia had a powwow and decided that I was going to attend their alma mater, Syracuse University. My guidance counselor bluntly stated that I shouldn't waste my time applying there because my grades weren't high enough. I thought he was also about to recommend that I attend nail school before I flew out of his cubicle. After that, I gave the guidance counselor the serious vapors.

Teachers generally frowned upon students auditioning for professional work, as they thought that it would distract them from mastering the craft. When casting directors from the television program *Star Search* sought young talent, I was strongly urged to audition. The night before the audition, my boyfriend, Ronald, pissed me off.

My friend Bernie had introduced me to her brother Ronald when I was in the tenth grade. Ronald was the greatest boyfriend any naive sixteen-year-old girl could ever want. He was short, but handsome, with golden brown skin and a slim body. He was popular and wore the freshest creased Lee jeans. He was four years older than me and came from a good family that originated from Dominica. Sometimes he would escort me to and from school. He would meet me at 6:30 A.M. every morning at the 30th Avenue train station in Astoria, where I would catch the N train. And he would be standing there on the platform in the cold. He never would come back through the turnstile because that would mean he would have to pay another fare when I arrived. He was even out there on days when I wouldn't go to school, and my friends would laugh. "Tarsha didn't tell you? She not going to school today."

He encouraged me to do well academically, and on the weekends we would always have dinner or do something special. He was enrolled at New York Technical in a two-year program and lived in the basement of his family's home, with a separate entrance. Our first Easter together was special, as I met his entire family. His mother and father and siblings were very welcoming.

Ronald was the first boy that I had sexual intercourse with. The experience was painful, bloody, and messy. Because I had been in effect a virgin—not counting the ten-second debacle with Shamaine—I didn't know how to get my sexual needs fulfilled. Most of the time, as Ronald snoozed like a satisfied breast-fed newborn baby, I just lay there thinking, *Daag! Is this all there is?*

Ronald was a member of the Turn Out Brothers, consisting of Christopher Reid, Christopher Martin (these two would later be known as Kid 'n Play) and Hurby "Luv Bug" Azor. Hurby had to create a rap group as a project for a class at the Center of Media Arts, a college that offered an audio production curriculum. Ronald recommended Bernie, Crystal—a singer/dancer from the school—and me to be members of Hurby's project. We were called the Choice MCs and rehearsed every weekend. We later performed wherever we could find a stage, to develop our showmanship. But the week before we were going to debut as headliners at a school talent show, I resigned because I needed to concentrate on my college applications and spend more time doing my school-work. Starting from scratch, Hurby scrambled to find a replacement group, and recruited two coworkers at Sears. They were Sandy Denton and Cheryl James. Hurby completed his school project and became the brain behind the trailblazing sensation Salt-N-Pepa.

Who knew?

The friendship between Bernie, Crystal, and me became strained after the Choice MCs dissolved. At school, Bernie and another class-mate, Kim, spread rumors that I was "talking about them." Among immature, adolescent girls, the most cardinal sin ever was to "talk about" someone else, although everyone did it. The social network among girls and women in general is so fragile that even the appear-ance of a slight can cause widespread hysteria. One day you're the best blood sisters and suddenly after lunch you have a fire-eating bitter enemy. And based upon a "she said/she said/and you know what else she said/and then she said" rumor, I was suddenly guilty without a chance to mount a defense, guilty before proven innocent.

Bernie made it her business to destroy by any means necessary my relationship with her brother Ronald. She no longer invited me to their home. And that hurt, because Bernie and I were friends before Ronald and I got together. And the closer Ronald and I became, the angrier Bernie became, especially when he would buy me fly clothes. And because sugar-and-spice girls talk about each other, Bernie ma-nipulated delusional girls into rolling their eyes and whispering be-hind my back. The stress was driving me batty, to the point where I would snap at teachers and my parents, and isolate myself, sobbing in my bedroom.

The night before my *Star Search* audition, Ronald and I attended a talent show, where I watched with my mouth hanging open as his sister and some other girls performed a routine that I had created. To make matters worse, Ronald ignored the fact that I was angry and kept leaving me alone and attending to their needs. As we rode home on the subway, I turned the tables on him, and ignored him just as he had ignored me that evening. Standing in the middle of the packed C train, gripping the steel rail, Ronald grew frustrated, and tried to make me have a conversation with him. In his mind, I was supposed to jump when he wanted me to. But when I had needs to be met, Ronald was nowhere to be found. Suddenly, as I stared into space, Ronald slapped me with an open hand across my face. The blow stung and the shock of Ronald's action brought tears to my eyes. The other passengers saw what he had done, but continued with their conversations.

Rubbing my cheek, I remained calm until I got home to Astoria, with Ronald tagging behind me. When I reached the front of my building, I saw some thuggy guys, who I knew in passing, hanging out on the benches. I ran to them and babbled what Ron had done. Immediately, they jumped off of the bench and stepped to a retreating Ronald, who turned on his Puma sneakers and jetted back to the train station. My thuggy protectors never caught Ronald. He phoned the next day, after I had arrived home from school.

"I can't believe you had them chase me. What I did was one thing, but it was between me and you. You know how those niggas are. Now I'm never gonna come back out there." But of course he did. In his backward way of thinking, he was the victim. And no matter how badly he treated me, I was to protect him at all costs.

During the audition that morning, I sang "Saving All My Love for You," but I knew that I didn't meet the standards of the *Star Search* talent buyers.

Ronald never physically hit me again.

"Tarsha is a ho! Don't speak to her! Ha! Ha! Ha!" Crystal, a big bubble-eyed chick from Rochdale Village, jumped on the Get Tarsha bandwagon with her taunts. I tried hard to ignore her, until one day I lost my temper.

"Tarsha is a ho! Everybody gets a turn with her! Ha! Ha! Ha!" she yelled when I passed her as she rode the down escalator. Enraged, I did an about-face and literally ran up the down escalator and unleashed the whooping of a lifetime on her. When the fight was broken up, the principal didn't discipline me, because witnesses said that she started it. Crystal was immediately expelled for fighting and violating academic probation.

"There is absolutely no way that Ronald doesn't know that his sister is involved! I'm telling you, he's behind it! He could put a stop to it if he really wanted to," my mother exclaimed. Alyce called Ronald's mother to complain about Bernie's spreading manipulative lies. Mrs. Lawrence listened but was in total denial about her daughter's behavior. According to her, neither Bernie nor Ronald could do any wrong. I must be imagining it all.

At first, my parents liked Ronald. He honored the curfew that my mother established. He arrived to pick me up on time and brought me home early. If we were going to be late, Ronald called my mother, and often she didn't mind extending the curfew, because he was a respectful guy. At two years and counting, we were a real couple. We were both intense Scorpios and when it was good it was very good. And when it was bad, it was very bad. But it was becoming apparent to my mother that his loyalty extended to his family first, which was admirable, but not when it brought harm on me. Ronald was either unwilling or unable to take a stand in my defense.

I had lost weight. Sleep became impossible. Often I lay wide-awake for nights on end just thinking about the possibility of another confrontation. Sleeping pills were prescribed. Bernie's friends would pass me singing The O'Jays's hit single "Back Stabbers": ". . . they smile in your face . . ." It wasn't that I was afraid of anyone, but when I should have been concentrating on my falling grades, I had flashbacks of the blows that I'd leveled against Crystal. Though my friend Tanya was supportive, she was as helpful as the cameraman who videotaped Rodney King's beat-down. *Shoot, put down the camera and help!*

About a week after the fight, my old friend Riggie from the Astoria Projects, who was now attending Music & Art, tapped on the window of my social studies class, signaling for me to join her in the hallway. "Crystal and 'em are gonna jump you after school today. I gotta get back to class, but here, wear this," Riggie said, shoving in my hand a metal ring with a hook. Riggie *would* happen to have a metal ring in her possession. That girl was always ready for some violence to jump off. Sighing, I braced myself for an ambush.

Sure enough, five girls wearing brass knuckles waited for me across the street from school. Those cowards followed behind me, yanking my hair. My friend Tanya, who was chicken to the core, squeezed my arm so hard, I thought a blood vessel would burst. When she and I walked fast, the girls trailing us sped up, until I was tired of playing with them and whirled around and dropped my book bag, and balled up my fists just like my mother had taught me.

With tunnel vision, all I concentrated on was Crystal, who obviously had sustained enough brain damage to believe that I had not really whooped her. Her expelled ass wanted some more. This time I beat her so bad that the hook from the silver metal ring dug under her eye and left a permanent black eye. My fury was so precise and concentrated that when Crystal's friends yanked out a big clump of my hair, I didn't even notice and sustained no other injuries. Big, black Shaynii, who no one would fuck with, happened to come through the tunnel just then and broke up the fight, handing me my clump of hair.

When my mother complained to administrators about the fight within yards of the school grounds, the response was, "Oh, it's just a girls' fight."

My mother pressed charges in Family Court against the girls involved and we used the clump of hair as evidence during the trial. Crystal was sentenced to a juvenile detention center. Pam's mother was a cop and hired a lawyer, who arranged a plea deal and probation. Melody, who was notorious for following behind the wrong leader, took the fall for everybody, because her mother wasn't around to advocate for her.

After that I was forbidden to see Ronald. Depressed and angry, I decided that I was going to punish Alyce and Sonny for keeping me away from him. I resented their not believing I'd be able to handle the situation on my own, though I hadn't given any indication that I could.

Sonny eventually suggested that my mother and I should go to a child psychologist for family therapy. He was sick of the arguments between Alyce and me, though her focus on me improved their relationship a great deal. Why he didn't attend the therapy as well, I don't know. I continued to violate Alyce and Sonny's orders to stay away from Ronald by secretly writing him letters. He didn't respond until I phoned him, and we began finding secret places to see each other. In my mind, what my parents didn't know wouldn't hurt them—that is, until my boss from Burger King called and asked if I could work an extra shift.

"What? She's supposed to be there!" Alyce was furious.

When I arrived home, my mother went to war. She was so angry, her body shook.

But I now know that behind her profanity-laced tirade was a mother who was afraid for the life of her daughter yet felt powerless to do anything about it. And I was too young and stupid to appreciate it.

The punishment came swift. I was restricted to the house and not allowed to go out or receive telephone calls. I flipped out. I screamed. I cried. I stomped out of the kitchen into my bedroom and sobbed, but now it was a deeper cry. I felt my heart was being ripped out of me without anesthesia. *I don't know how to fix everything. She always wins,* I thought. And of course, I never took responsibility for deceiving my parents. Instead it was Alyce's fault. She wasn't giving me the space to work it out with this boy/man. And since she wouldn't listen to why I needed to be with Ronald, the only answer would be for me to commit suicide.

But first I called Burger King and told them to take me off of the schedule. I thought, *If in fact I do die, I don't want to lose my job.* Even in death I wanted to be responsible. Burger King refused to take me off the schedule, but they can never say on my epitaph that I didn't call in. Resolved not to wake up and to scare my mother so she would respect my feelings, I swallowed a palm full of red sleeping pills.

The next morning, I awoke drugged and still took my ass to work. Ronald and I continued as a couple, despite his inability to protect me against his sister. In my warped sense of justification, I both resented Ronald and believed that I deserved his abuse. And my parents didn't hide their disdain for him, but they gave up fighting with me about it.

My biological father, Billy, called to check on me. "If you need to go to the next level and you need somebody to get gully, just let me know. We can handle them."

I sought a safer outlet, in the arms of Joseph, a married NYC bus driver, who was ten years my senior, and worst of all, cheap. He got off sexually by bedding high school girls, like me, during his work shift. I was easily flattered by the attentions of an older man. Especially an older man who talked smack about Ronald. Joseph was safer than Billy to unleash my heartbreak to because I knew he wasn't going to do anything but run his mouth. Senior year, I applied for early entry to the education department at Syracuse University, and was rejected. My sisters suggested that I reapply to the music department since that was going to be my area of concentration. Though I'd already been accepted by the University of Buffalo, I wanted to continue the family legacy at Syracuse. So I submitted my audition tapes from Music & Art, and at the last minute, I received a letter of acceptance. I had loved visiting my sisters there and meeting their college friends and I looked forward to having my own experience.

During a dental exam to pass my physical for college, the dentist noted an abnormal reading on my X-ray and made a referral to a specialist. After conducting a biopsy, the oral surgeon diagnosed the spots on the X-ray as amelobastoma, a tumor that had invaded my jawbone. Besides occasional swelling in some people, there are no symptoms. Through an office procedure, the oral surgeon removed the growth and I was able to return to school the next morning, though I had swelling.

Graduation morning, Ronald arrived early to drive me to Lincoln Center, where the graduation ceremonies were to be held. My family met us there, with my mother glaring and daring Ronald to leave her side to join his family. After the ceremony, I received congratulatory hugs from everyone and left to retrieve my actual diploma. Ron, welcoming the opening, slipped away to join his family. I needed to get home and finish packing because I was leaving the next morning for Syracuse to attend the SummerStart program.

A white full-length limousine idled alongside Lincoln Center on 66th Street. I received a page from its passenger.

It was Slick Rick, in his entire gold-and-diamond-bejeweled splendor.

Earlier in my senior year, I had gotten a mysterious package that contained flowers and an embroidered Mickey Mouse sweatshirt, mailed from Universal Studios in Orlando, Florida. Later Slick Rick revealed that he had been the secret admirer sending the gifts. His heartfelt gesture meant a great deal to me and came when I was in the depths of depression. Slick Rick and I spent all evening at dinner, catching up on each other's lives. The city was still rocking from his hits "La Di Da Di" and "The Show." And he had been on a nationwide tour with rapper Doug E. Fresh. On Slick Rick's order, the limo driver gave me one last tour of the stunning Manhattan skyline, with a stop at my father's house in Jersey City. Though Slick Rick and I only had a friendship, I treasured the generosity he showed me during my high school senior year. Rick always brought me joy, and never drama.

When I finally arrived home after midnight, a sniveling Ronald was at the other end of the telephone receiver. "Where were you? Who were you with on your last night in town?" I was indifferent to his feelings. Ronald had allowed his sister to make the last two years of my life miserable. I refused to answer any of his questions, excused myself, and finished packing to travel into the next chapter of my life.

SYRACUSE

Just as Rachel and I had lathered in Bengay ointment to recuperate from a grueling conditioning class, there were screams in the corridor. "Eeeeeeeeeee!!! Basketball players are on the floor!! Omigod! I just saw them down the hall! Omigod!!" Nonchalantly, my roommate, Rachel, pushed the door so that it was slightly ajar, just as white girls, who had been fully clothed ten seconds earlier, stripped naked and wrapped themselves in towels and pretended they just happened to be on their way to or from the shower so they could flaunt themselves.

I didn't move. Not because I didn't want to, but because I physically couldn't. That afternoon, Rachel and I had run drills, done squats and push-ups, working muscles I didn't even know I had. Even my eyeball muscles hurt, I was so sore. Rachel had signed us up for a conditioning class that was specifically designed for the football team. Of course, I was notified of that little detail after I had dragged myself to the showers.

Freshman year at Syracuse University, and I was having the time of my life. My second-floor mates were friendly, adventurous, and just as happy to be out from under their parents as I was. They had very interesting backgrounds and were from all over the world. Our floor was the "It" floor and often became one gigantic pajama party. It was a struggle to get to class on time by myself, after relying on my mother's constant yelling, "This is the last time I'm gonna call you, Tarsha! The last time!"

Now I was responsible for when I ate, and if I ate at all, and whether I registered for and attended classes. Unlike anytime before, my life was completely my responsibility.

My first roommate was very fucking corny and hated black music. Her midget boyfriend thought it was his responsibility to get up in my business. "Her radio is too loud." "Why isn't she at class?" Thankfully, Miss Tight-Ass moved out midsemester, and my friend Rachel moved in. Together we were declared the Two New Hotties on campus.

"Hey, Shorty!" a deep voice said, tapping on the door.

"Are you expecting company?" I said, rubbing my thighs with a new layer of ointment. Rachel opened the door as a 6'10" guy prepared to knock again, enveloping the entire door frame. Behind him was another long, tall boy, with towel-wrapped white girls traipsing back and forth, bewildered as to why they were being ignored.

I never appreciated the fact that Syracuse University was an athletic school. On our campus, all athletes, followed by frat boys, considered themselves gods. And their campus groupies agreed. In the cafeteria, I would notice boys with big necks sitting at tables on one side of the room, but I never paid them the kind of attention they were used to.

I was a popular freshman and genuinely interested in making new friends. However, my interest in others was based upon personality as opposed to what kind of ball a person sported. So I never knew how Derrick Coleman, who was en route to being an NBA superstar, ended up at my door that evening, and was not deterred by my aroma of ointment.

Derrick was born in Mobile, Alabama, but reared by his grandmother in Detroit. He was that rare combination of Southern gentleman and city dweller. He was quiet, but we had fun, simple times, an innocent relationship. Though we looked great together, we had a forced chemistry straight out of central casting; Derrick, the wildly popular basketball player, and me, the popular freshman, who brought flavor to the music department.

The summer after freshman year Derrick invited me to visit him in Detroit, but Alyce and Sonny wanted me to join them on a trip to Hawaii. Combined with forced chemistry and the fact that his roommate, Stevie, was pushing up on me, Derrick and I decided to be just great friends. I was later thrilled when he won Big East Rookie of the Year honors in 1987.

Meanwhile, Ronald, who was then attending Howard University, kept blowing up my telephone at the dorm. He still thought that he had a chance in hell to get back with me. He tried everything, from sending me money to airline tickets to fly home, which I cashed and spent with a quickness. He refused to accept how his lack of loyalty affected me. He had rocked my world. If he had put his sister Bernie in check, I wouldn't have had the battles that I did, especially with a so-called boyfriend as a passive bystander. At first I tried to be polite, until he acted like I was his to possess. I bugged. "Look, I'm tired of dealing with this old shit! I have a great new life! Stop calling here, and leave me the fuck alone! I don't want to be with you!"

And that's how I ended our relationship . . . by rocking his world.

There must have been 50 million steps to climb to enter the Crouse School of Music every day. The actual building was constructed like a castle. When you reached the top, you were so winded, you could barely sing. Once you entered the building, you were in an entirely different world than the other parts of the campus. There was hushed silence. People spoke in low tones. The only explosion of noise that was heard was the tinkering of piano keys, vocal rehearsals, or faculty recitals. Socially, I felt very isolated in this building. The school of music was all white except for Shawn, the only other black student; Shawn competed against me competitively, as if she should be annointed as the "star" black student. Even so, I much preferred going to classes where there were black kids who got their work done but still maintained their style.

Music instructor Donna Miller and I used to battle. She would counter my New York–accented excuses with her Southern belle–twanged orders to continue two hours of intense vocal releases and exercises, without whining. Voice instruction is the most intense that a vocalist can endure. During class, its up to you to create a balancing act with the piano and to technically and emotionally perform foreign classical music and operas. I also learned intricate scales and vocal exercises. I had to be extremely focused, and always discovered some new shit in myself. She pushed me to discipline myself. And Ms. Miller wore me out, but successfully guided me to face faculty at stress-inducing recitals. Even though she knew that I wanted to be an R&B singer, she made the classical and opera forms of music relevant to me, a girl from the projects of Astoria, Queens.

At first, I was turned off by opera because I didn't understand the language. "What are they saying?" I would ask Ms. Miller.

"You may not understand what they're saying, but can't you sense the emotion? It's less about interpreting the words and more about interpreting the meaning." Opera lost its drudgery as the brilliance of divas Leontyne Price and Jessye Norman became part of my repertoire. I began listening to opera with my heart instead of my brain; only then could I truly understand. It resonated with me because there was always a fight to learn, and that mirrored the challenges in my life. Everything I have achieved, I have had to fight for . . . at every level of my life—I always had to fight, but once I got through it, I always felt I had won, from finding and landing a job, to auditioning for Music & Art and getting accepted, to being accepted to Syracuse when I probably should have only gotten into Tarrytown. I felt obligated not to let Ms. Miller down. We battled, but everything she threw at me I nailed. And sang with conviction because I knew I sang the classics and operas technically and phonetically correct. In time, I would only select the most difficult French arias, such as *Après un Rêve* by Romaine Bussine. Ms. Miller invested in me, and I responded by doing more than my best in her class.

But just like at Music & Art, it was difficult for me to care about courses I felt had nothing to do with me being an R&B singer.

"**M**om, put Daddy on the phone." And Alyce would go, "Ah, man, she's about to ask you for something."

"I ain't got no money, so what is it?"

"I need money for my phone bill."

"I just sent you money."

"I know, but it's all gone."

"How much do you need?"

"Fifty."

"Okay, I'll send it out when I get paid on Thursday, but don't tell your mother." Though I loved my independence, I loved Sonny and Alyce for their support of me. They may not have had much, but what they had or could get was mine if I needed it. Often Sonny would wire me money without my asking. Sometimes I would call them just to hear their voices after I returned from class.

"Hey, why don't y'all come hang out with us up at Skytop?" Ben asked with his smiling frat brother Don, on the prowl for freshmen lovelies and new pledges when they strolled into the lobby of my dorm. Both were in their junior year and members of Omega Psi Phi fraternity. Rumor had it that they collected women, but that didn't phase me, because they were handsome, older, and lived on South Campus, which was the dream of every newly freed freshman like me. South Campus had beautiful town houses, where you felt grown-up, like you were living in your own house, but without your parents.

By the second semester, I had allowed myself to serve on Ben's sandwich-and-sex committee. Rachel leased an apartment on South Campus to be near Don. When I asked about doing the same, my mother refused. Anything I was dying to do probably wasn't a good idea, she (rightly) thought. Plus, I was still struggling with my grades, when I wasn't distracted with Ben. With him I felt like I was a chore. After spending the night with him, he would drop me off, in his car, closer to his class than mine. He had no conversation other than "Did you bring me a sandwich?" and "Come break me off." But when we returned from Christmas break and he had perched another girl's photo on top of his bed, I kicked him to the purple-and-gold curb.

"Is Tarsha gonna sing?" That was a popular question around Syracuse University, especially at the black Greek fraternity and sorority parties. From what I saw, I admired members of the fraternities and sororities. Besides what they say about community service in their handbooks, they always gave the best parties. There was no party like a black Greek party on the yard. Audrey had pledged Sigma Gamma Rho, and Marci, Alpha Kappa Alpha, so I looked forward to entering Greek life and had my heart set on AKA.

After hearing me sing at an Alpha Phi Alpha party, Ernie, a brilliant keyboardist, introduced himself. We became instant friends. Ernie knew everything about music. He inspired and kept me sharp with classical music, and showed me another way to break down an Angela Wimbush song. Ernie explained, "There is a connective line between classical and R&B music. Just because it's R&B, it's no different. You still need to interpret the song in your own way and put the breath marks in the right place."

After I finished singing, Rachel nonchalantly introduced me to a 6'1" Kappa junior on academic probation named Bryant, who was also from Queens. He had seen me around with Ben, appreciated my singing, but thought that I was off-limits. This distinguished young man was charming and a good dresser and I began auditioning for a position as his girlfriend the second half of my freshman year. By this time, I craved to be loved by a man of my own. Rachel and Don were engaged in a serious relationship, so I was rarely able to hang out with her. And arias, the classics, and academics were cute, but I needed the warm arms of a man around me. Bryant was a suitable choice, as he reflected my low self-esteem. The more aloof he was, the more determined I was to prove that I was worthy of his love. The higher the hoop he raised, the higher I jumped. Behind his suave, handsome demeanor was a deeply troubled young man. I knew what he told me about his abusive mother and deceased father. But I didn't have an appreciation for how his home life affected him, and would soon affect me.

During our late-night conversations, Bryant would share that though his mother was a born-again Christian, she'd dumped her hostility about everything on him. Soon she adopted her young nephew, who was a few years younger than Bryant. Bryant and his cousin/adopted brother were often severely beaten by his mother. One day, Bryant saw iron cord marks on the little boy's body and reported his mother's alleged actions to the police. They believed her denials and didn't pursue a case against her; Bryant was put out, never allowed to return home, not even for vacations from college—nothing. Bryant was disowned.

One morning, during spring break, he arrived at 5:00 A.M. at my parents' apartment because he had slept on a park bench and had no place else to go.

Soon after we met, our pattern of nightly fucks without commitment began. Unhappy about what was taking place, I confronted Bryant about his lack of commitment, and he was . . . er, non-committal. My frustration grew out of the fact that unless Bryant was in my bed, I had no idea where he was—or who he was with, for that matter. Feelings of powerlessness affected my course work, as well as my music. When I was late for the tenth time for rehearsing for an upcoming show, Ernie pounded the keys of the piano in frustration. "All right, what's going on? We can't get through this until you get past that!" Ernie was always right. I decided that if Bryant wanted to be wild and free, then so could I.

"Hello, how are you?" the finest man at Syracuse asked while we were reading the community bulletin board in the student union. "I'm Paris Davis." Every girl east of the Mississippi knew Paris Davis. He was so fine that your mouth almost stopped working when he bedazzled you with his smile. Next thing I knew, I was having an evening of great conversation and quality male companionship. The tongue-waggers on campus, of course, felt the need to report back to Bryant.

Bryant was not pleased. "You ain't no fucking good . . . out disrespecting me with some other nigga!"

"Wait just a fuckin' minute, you're the one running the streets, fucking with all kind of bitches and rubbing my nose in it . . . not me, Bryant!" Then it dawned on me. My so-called date with Paris was Bryant's excuse to stop seeing me or to continue disrespecting me. "Look, you do what you think you gotta do," I said calmly. Bryant looked at me as if I had taken leave of my senses. I was no longer willing to argue with him. "Do what you gotta do," I said, flipping open a file of sheet music.

One night at a party at the Kappa Alpha Psi house, Bryant, who was high on weed, had holed himself in his room with Kimberly, who was notorious for sleeping around. Mario, her boyfriend, and I were downstairs, getting antsy and curious about what Bryant and Kimberly were doing behind closed doors. Finally, I marched to Bryant's room. When I barged in, he claimed that he was trying to set her up, to prove to Mario that she couldn't be trusted. Bryant knew that I didn't approve of his game-playing, and it escalated into a loud argument. With his frat brothers and other partygoers trying to restrain him, Bryant picked me up and threw me, barely clothed, outside into the snow. Witnessing my embarrassment, his roommates let me back inside and protected me in one of their bedrooms, while Bryant slept off his high. Having grown up in a household where frequent fighting and personal sacrifice was a norm, I never saw it as cause to go our separate ways.

Bryant would not have survived in school without me sharing half of the money my mother sent me for groceries and school supplies. Still, he squandered my generosity and smoked weed, hung out, and eventually flunked most of his classes. Bryant expected me to run after him, but I did not. I had other problems. The dean's office notified me that if my grade point average didn't improve, I couldn't return to Syracuse University. I threw myself into my studies and was able to raise my grade point average one point above the 2.0 requirement. I regretted having to withdraw my application to pledge AKA, but determined that I would definitely apply again next year.

Over the summer, at home in Queens some of my former girl enemies now welcomed me; either because they had matured or because they didn't have to worry that I was going to fuck their man. I got as many jobs as I could through temp agencies and bagged groceries at the project supermarket. The trip to Hawaii with Alyce and Sonny was great. As I grew older, our relationship continued to improve. My parents boasted to their friends, when they thought that I was out of earshot, how proud they were of me.

There was no word from Bryant the entire summer.

FIVE

COMING TO TERMS

Jonesy's Juice:

Carmen Bryant: In 1997, when Nas was with Carmen, tell-all author and his baby's mother, the press asked Nas and me to pose for a photo during the Ed Lover Celebrity Roast. When Carmen saw us, she became so outraged that she stormed out of the ballroom . . . crying.

Later that same night, Busta's baby's mother saw Busta and me pose for another photo. And she ran out and started crying.

One Stormy Night. Two Cryin' Bitches.

When my sophomore year began, Bryant returned with a brand-new attitude. Apparently, he'd had time to think over the summer and had decided that he wanted to be with me. I responded by giving him my body, money, and groceries. I often traveled in the snow on the bus to visit Bryant with three book bags, carrying books, clothes for the next day, and groceries to feed him and his roommate. To break me out of my euphoria, the campus grapevine was jumping with the news that Bryant had been tapping the ass of his ex-girlfriend Lisa. Stevie Thompson, Derrick's roommate, was sick of hearing about Bryant every time I caught him in some shit. "You so caught up in that no-good nigga . . . He's right up there with Lisa! And all you can do is think about him? He ain't thinking about you! Call me when you ready!" Stevie's words stung so hard, I didn't know whether to blink back tears or let them fall. Stevie had been very clear that he cared about me. Anytime I needed something, Stevie was there, Johnny-on-the-spot. Looking back now I wish I believed that I could have accepted the affections of a really nice brother. His generous support did not mirror how I felt about myself, though.

"Tarsha, Sonny is in the hospital. But nothing serious," Audrey said. I caught the next ride to New York City. When Sonny lifted his eyelids, I was eating his lime Jell-O. A smile spread across his face. "Whatchu doin' here?" he asked.

"I'm here to see you, Daddy!" I said, running my hand softly across his forehead.

Sonny was never in great health. He took pills for gout. His joints and feet would swell, causing him excruciating pain. When doctors would order him to stop drinking and to minimize the rich foods and keep his weight down, he would placate them with "You right, Doc!" until he passed his employment physical, and then he'd go right back to eating the foods that brought on the gout in the first place, ballooning back to 275 Santa Claus belly pounds.

It was great spending time with Sonny and being away from the drama at college. When I returned to campus, I received glowing praise from the music faculty at the mid-term recital.

"Sonny is dead, Tarsha. Sonny passed away. Come home." The nightmare kept repeating itself. Audrey was on the other end of my telephone receiver at 7:00 A.M. on October 19, 1987. The day the man who was my daddy made his transition.

I screamed, reaching more octaves than I had ever done during recitals. Rachel and Don ran into the room, wiping weariness from their eyes. "My daddy's dead. My daddy's dead." It was the first parental death among any of my friends. No one knew what to say, rubbing my shoulder as I sat on my suitcase blowing my nose. My friend Helena drove me in her gray Subaru to Queens. Much of what occurred that day still remains a blur to me. Bryant arranged to meet me later in New York.

When I arrived at the apartment, no one was there. My knees bent when I realized that Sonny would not return there, where he had built a life for us. I walked around the spotless kitchen, mindlessly opening the refrigerator. All of the unhealthy foods he loved were sitting on the first and second shelf, waiting for him. I loved Sonny, and he knew it. I am so thankful that I was with him the week before. Sonny Tharpe was a good man. And he was my daddy. A written note was left on the kitchen counter: "We're at Astoria General. Here is money. Take a cab."

Sonny had been released from the hospital since the last time I saw him. One week later, and days before his impending retirement, Sonny rose to go the bathroom, preparing for work. My mother heard a loud crash as Sonny hit the radiator, gripping his heart. She dialed 911. Her cries awoke Miss Eunice from across the hall. Miss Eunice knew that unlike other emotional scenes in our apartment over the years, this was the one to get involved with.

Minutes ticked away, and still no ambulance in sight, Miss Eunice continued to pump Sonny's heart until she slowed, then stopped. "Alyce, I think he's gone, baby."

Miss Eunice held my mother tightly to prevent her from completely unraveling. In fact, even though my sisters and I were not there, Miss Eunice held us together. She was our rock.

"You and me are just alike, and you are going to be fine," I whispered, and hugged my mother the morning of Sonny's funeral. She had reverted back into a little girl. As expected, her eyes were swollen and red from tears. One moment she was having breakfast, and the next she had to be held down by my sisters or me so she wouldn't injure herself. We were all exhausted, but Alyce had to deal with Sonny's family, many of whom she had never met. His family wanted to control what was going to be in the obituary, who was going to conduct the eulogy and what was going to be served at the reception. They also wanted Sonny shipped down South. But of course nobody offered a nickel to pay for anything. During one conference call, in which I participated, his niece Betty said to my mother, "You did this to my uncle and you are going to pay." I interjected, "I don't know who you think you are, but don't you ever talk to my mother like that."

Before the ceremony began, a dark-complexioned woman and three crying kids entered the funeral home, signed the guest book, and sat in Sonny's family's section in the rear. Curious as to whom she was, I walked over and read the guest book. In a deliberate print, the name read: "Brenda Tharpe."

I was stunned.

When I lifted my jaw off the gold-plated podium, this Brenda was standing next to me with tears gleaming behind her eyes. "Are you Nikki? I'm Brenda, and these are your father's kids. Sonny said that you would be the understanding one, and that I could talk to you. And I never wanted him to leave your mother . . . I told him I wanted him to stay with her."

I looked over at my mother, Audrey, and Marcia, who were unaware that some shit was getting ready to jump off. I said, "Bitch, if you don't get those snotty-nosed kids out of this funeral home—"

"But—"

"Get out! My mother doesn't want to have anything to do with you and neither do we . . . and these are not my brother and sisters. Nor will they ever be acknowledged as such. Now, get the fuck out!" I hissed.

My mother never knew that Brenda came to Sonny's funeral. I

wondered if she was the same Brenda that they argued about years earlier. Whether what Brenda was saying was true or not held little relevance to me. It was my duty to protect my mother and honor Sonny. I
knew him only as a father, not as a man. But I thought it was the purest
form of selfishness for her to characterize herself as a martyr. If Sonny
had wanted to be with her ass, he would have been man enough to
make that happen.

After Sonny had been memorialized down South, my mother tried
her best to keep her sanity. Still, some moments were better than others. Alyce got drunk and tore through the house, fucking with the first
person she saw, which always happened to be Audrey.

"Get up! You're not supposed to sleep until twenty-four hours after
the body dies because you have to stay up with the spirit until it passes
into heaven." Audrey and I needed sister time, and we were lying in
our mother's bed long after the last guest had departed.

"Mom, I'm tired. I been up all day and all night," Audrey whined.

"I said get up!" our mother snapped.

Audrey didn't move, nor did I. Though Alyce didn't address Audrey by name, my eldest sister was usually the point person for our
mother's tirades. Seeing that Audrey hadn't moved, Alyce pulled out
her gun. We weren't going to launch an investigation at that time as to
whether or not it was loaded.

"Get out of my muthafuckin' house right now. You don't think I
won't use this?"

Audrey was devastated. Part of her spirit left her body. No child
ever expects that they would be placed in harm's way by a parent. My
mother got what she wanted. She was able to control the situation.
Audrey rose, packed, and bolted to her own apartment. After Audrey left, Alyce threatened to smash my face in my birthday cake,
which a neighbor had been kind enough to bake. As we struggled,
Alyce punched me in the face. Startled, I punched her right the fuck
back. And she decided to leave me alone.

The next week I returned to Syracuse University.

"Look at my transcript. Does this look okay?" Several people reviewed it. I'd just changed it, forging a better grade, from 2.3 to 2.5, to qualify for the upcoming pledge season for Alpha Kappa Alpha sorority. Forging wasn't out of the ordinary, as it was commonly known that many people had also "improved" their transcript. Thus, my rationale was, *What's good for them is good for me*. My mistake was that I told too many blabbermouthed people, and the AKAs called a meeting to address my false transcript.

"Everybody knows about the transcript, so don't go in there trying to play it off . . . like you don't know what it is," Bryant advised. When I arrived at the AKA meeting, I felt like I were in front of a military tribunal determined to issue swift justice and my public embarrassment was to be punitive damages.

"I'm so disappointed to think that you were my friend and I've vouched for you all year," Terry, who had pledged the year before, whined.

"Whatever!" I responded, waiting for evidence that I should be intimidated. These corny, shallow, and non-stepping bitches had been down with changing grades for years. And now Terry was pleading ignorance. "Please!"

It all dawned on me at once. This attempt to censure me wasn't about the change of grades. It was about Lisa, Bryant's ex-girlfriend. Lisa's sorority sisters had watched her cry every single night while they pledged. And in their minds, I was the source of her tears. My application was denied. The non-stepping, snooty broads went on to pledge girls who were already on academic probation. Those girls needed one another to feel like something, and their lies were exposed when their little chapter was subsequently suspended for hazing.

After we got past Lisa and other issues, Bryant gradually got himself together. He worked to earn his own tuition and had a 4.0 grade point average. We became like a married couple enrolled in college. If Ronald was my first love, Bryant was definitely my second. We would drive to school in the morning, meet for lunch or dinner, entertain mutual friends and support each other's study goals. Bryant showed that he believed in me. When I sought his advice on any given issue, he would listen carefully, give it some thought, and then return with helpful feedback. He was very supportive.

While hanging out one weekend in Harlem with Tichina Arnold after a performance during Apollo Theater's Amateur Night, I found an application for the Ms. New York Beauty Pageant and entered. After going through so much turmoil at Syracuse and with Sonny's death, I sang the Stephanie Mills version of "If I Were Your Woman," garnering first runner-up. The prize was a full-length fur coat and a cash prize, for which I had to sue the producer in Civil Court for breach of contract. But I used my appearance in the pageant to leverage bookings at other venues so that I could continue to develop my craft.

My mother began experiencing pain in her neck. Her private physician diagnosed her with a pinched nerve, and for two years she wore a neck brace. A year later, Alyce received a second opinion, from another doctor, and was diagnosed with throat cancer. After radiation treatment and surgery, the illness went into remission. She never lost her hair; in fact, it grew very long. She was in great spirits and felt she had a second lease on life, traveling to visit Marcia in Kansas City and working for the first time in her life.

In December of 1990, the cancer returned and spread with a vengeance. The doctors gave her six months to live. Being away at college, I had no idea how bad my mother's illness was. Alyce told my sisters that she didn't want to worry me. Audrey would sit with her at night, because Momma was afraid to be alone. On the day of my graduation from Syracuse University, Bryant, Audrey, and her husband, Harold, applauded as I crossed the stage to accept my diploma. My mother was too ill to make the trip.

Six months to the day that her physicians had predicted, Alyce Scott Jones made her transition, on June 26, 1991.

When it comes to responding to a fact of life like death, people may mean well, but empty clichés are annoying, and when you're in mourning, someone saying "They are in a better place now" or "When it's your time, it's your time" just doesn't wash. How does anyone really know? People repeat the same old clichés that have been said to them.

"I'm so sorry, Tarsha," Bryant said. While my mother was in the hospital, Bryant had washed her and helped her to the bathroom, up until a week before her death. My father, Billy, attended the funeral carrying a cane, and didn't say one word.

I didn't fully appreciate the impact of my loss until I went to the housing office of Astoria Projects. The sad faces of the building staff still haunt me. "She never bothered anybody . . . she was a good woman," they said. Their condolences were so heartfelt, I realized that I experienced a shared loss with my sisters as well as our neighbors. Marcia stayed with Bryant and me for a while before returning to Kansas City. Then soon after Bryant returned to Syracuse to continue his studies. To be close to my mother, I slept in her bed, which still had her scent. The apartment became my mother's mausoleum. I refused to disturb her possessions for ten years. And I couldn't wait to fall asleep so I could dance with her in my dreams.

SIX

WHEN HE MOVED, I MOVED

Jonesy's Juice:

50 Cent: 50 Cent has overcome so much—his mother's murder, the alleged murderer taunting him, and backlash for not letting corporations pimp him. And now people hate on him. No one was checking for him back in the day, so don't act like he owes you anything. When he got the opportunity to shut things down, he did.

Fiddy sacrificed and kept at it.

In this get-it-quick society, 50 Cent is taking the time to build his empire. And I love the fact that he has not pigeonholed himself into one genre of entertainment. I also love that he incorporates other young, aspiring African-American artists in his projects.

My mother's passing left me devastated. I went through the motions of trying to get through the day, trying to mask my pain. Inside, I was both depressed and angry that she was gone. Living in the apartment that I grew up in, alone, did not brighten my mood. I gained weight and didn't take pride in my appearance the way I once had. I felt powerless to do anything about it, other than to constantly yank down my shirt over my expanding belly. In an act of frustration, I spontaneously chopped off my hair, as tears fell from my eyes. Now I know that my action was a metaphor. I hated the image of myself in the mirror. And I needed to suspend any connection to that girl who I felt held no value in the world. If nature abhors a vacuum, then my soul desperately tried to fill it.

Bryant was still at Syracuse University, but he would visit on weekends, checking on me. Because of my mother's death, I was so depressed that I couldn't muster the motivation to follow through on my plans to get my master's in music at Howard University. Without notifying the university, I never showed up. I worked for AT&T as a telephone operator to pay my rent. That job made me even more depressed because my singing career wasn't taking off as I had expected. My rent was $200 per month and my salary was $199 per week before taxes, so I had to learn how to do without and stretch the little money I had. It was a two-dollar-chicken-wings kind of time.

While I'd been away at college, my singing style had become more operatic. When I returned to New York City, the streets were pulsating with the first wave of a new music called hip-hop, and not the watered-down version I had heard at Syracuse. I had to make my voice reflective of the flavor that pulsated out of boom boxes and radios in Bed-Stuy, Jamaica, and Harlem. It was energizing, riding across the Queensborough Bridge into Manhattan, and hanging out with my friends along 125th Street, listening to new MCs or creating new beats and rhymes on the spot. The distraction helped to shake my depression.

Marcia had moved from Kansas City to Chicago with her husband. Audrey had eloped to Manhattan with a man my mother never approved of. Because I internalized my mother's wishes, Audrey's choice strained our relationship. And it really became strained when Audrey was to accompany me to an audition with the recording artist Omar

Chandler. As planned, when I got off work at AT&T, I called Audrey. She had changed her mind.

"My husband doesn't want me out on the street that late at night. You need to give up your dream to be a singer and get a nine-to-five job like regular people and stop trying to borrow money from me."

When a friend heard what was wrong and agreed to go with me to the audition. The disappointment from Audrey's abandonment made me sing in a way that moved everyone in the studio, including Omar Chandler himself. He hired me on the spot. Determined to use this experience to refocus on my music, I did not allow anyone to deter me from my dreams, even if they were family members.

Soon I caught a gig filling in for renowned studio vocalist Audrey Wheeler on Omar Chandler's hit single "This Must Be Heaven." And one for Travis "Spunk" Macklin. I also danced occasionally for rap artists Casanova Rudd and Super Lover Cee. But still, the next morning I was always right back at the AT&T switchboard, saying, "This is Tarsha. How may I help you?"

One fall afternoon in 1991, my running buddy Danielle Leathers, Spunk, and I had heard that we could use a Medicaid card to buy designer eyeglasses from Dr. Benjamin's, an optical store on 125th Street near Lenox Avenue, which was directly across from Men's Walkers, where fly guys bought their gator shoes, derbys and fedoras. As we were leaving Dr. Benjamin's ecstatic with our new find, Spunk kept looking across the street at a lean black man wearing sunglasses. Spunk said, "I'm going across the street. I know that nigga. I'm gonna hook you up."

And I'm like "Yea, whateva," not knowing what the hell he was talking about. Danielle and I remained where we were, leaning on Spunk's hoopdie. Spunk and this brother gave each other the black man handshake and chatted, while cars and trucks clogged the traffic artery leading to the Triborough Bridge. Finally, Spunk smiled and waved for us to join him. Weaving in and out of moving vehicles, I focused on who Spunk was talking to. My heart raced and I gulped when

I recognized the man who stared intently into my face, with a wry smile.

It was hip-hop legend Doug E. Fresh.

Before we could exchange pleasantries, Doug got right to the point. "Spunk said you sing."

No time for modesty now.

"Yeah, I sing," I replied, as I beat myself up for wearing jeans, sneakers, and a floppy velvet hat. I was not rocking anything but about three inches of new growth.

"Then sing something."

Blasting from the loudspeakers was an old Side B of a Denise Williams song. Holding my fist as if it were a microphone, like I had practiced in my bedroom mirror, I sang as if I were headlining my own HBO music special. Store customers formed a circle around us and gave me a warm ovation when I finished. Doug took note of the admiring smiles and the comments of "Go 'head, girl" from the customers.

"You sound good. You sound real good. And you were not nervous to sing on the spot," Doug said, licking his lips, giving me the once-over as we exchanged telephone numbers. Doug was the first real celebrity I had ever met. Even though it had been a while since he had released an album, I was in awe because he wanted to do business with me. Doug was the closest I had been to hip-hop royalty.

That weekend, Doug called. "Hey! This is Doug E. Fresh. We met the other day at Men's Walkers. Trying to catch up witchu."

Wow, he's calling me, I thought, as I rewound the answering-machine tape. Instead of returning his call, I phoned my friends, screaming, "He called! He called! He called!" Bryant, who was still up at school, was very happy for me. I even called people that I didn't like.

When I finally reached Doug, I gave him my address and he set a meeting time. And that was my first experience with Doug being three hours late for everything. As the hours passed until he finally arrived, it didn't matter that he was late. All that mattered was that Doug E. Fresh had come to see me.

From that moment, Doug and I connected on a different level. He wanted to know everything about me and not necessarily about the singing. He asked deep questions about family relationships and the kind of support I had from friends. He wanted to know what kind of a man Bryant was to me. "Does he treat you right?" My views on life were important to him. I told him about my music training and my determination to succeed in the record industry. I knew if I wanted to learn from him that I had to go with him everywhere. Every day I went with Doug to producer Barry Bee's house, listened to music and tried to suck up as much knowledge as I could. I watched and prepared. With Doug, I learned that if he leaves your sight, you might not connect again physically with him for another seven days. Your best bet was to park your car and get in his. So no matter where he was, you were. I saw what he saw. Met the people he knew. Plucked his brain for advice. Although Bryant listened the best he could, I was more enamored with the attention that Doug gave me. He helped me make sense of the loss of my mother. There are certain people that are able to provide you with wisdom that even the people closest to you are unable to. They live on a different plane and possess a higher level of understanding. For me, this was Doug.

When he moved, I moved.

"Look, Tarsha, I wanna add a girl to The Get Fresh Crew. And I'm thinking that person should be you," Doug said one morning on our way to Junior's for breakfast after Doug had come to see me perform at the Apollo Theater with Omar Chandler. "But you're gonna have to lose weight. You'll have to train and work like you never have before. You have to be willing to practice every night. And it's not gonna be easy."

The news of my association with Doug E. Fresh swept through the Astoria Projects like wildfire. Friends and strangers rooted for me, like I was their Prodigal Daughter.

Everything became a whirlwind.

I lived in the projects and worked nearby, now at Enterprise Rent-

A-Car. When my manager at Enterprise Rent-A-Car denied my request for time off, I quit. I had two months before I would join Doug, the production staff, musicians and The Get Fresh Crew in Los Angeles. Money was still an obstacle for me. I was left $35,000 in my mother's will. Marcia, who was the administrator of the estate, refused to give me the money unless it was an emergency. And to Marcia, this Doug nonsense was no emergency. When I explained my financial situation, Doug said, "If you believe in yourself, your bills will get paid. And I won't let you down."

There was no written contract defining our relationship. But in the back of my head, I knew there was a singer's union or AFTRA to protect me if something jumped off. So I flew to Los Angeles based upon his word. I was to support myself with the $500 I received for singing on Bust It Records and a $35 per diem, as well as my savings and prayers.

I didn't have time to catch my breath. The next thing I knew, I was being escorted to Doug's apartment suite in Los Angeles. When he opened his door and saw me, Doug smiled and said, "You made it. Welcome!"

Over his right shoulder, there was a girl lying in his bed. Doug didn't let her naked ass interrupt his excitement over seeing me. "The stylist has to pick you up some clothes. And the tailor has to make you a Get Fresh jacket." Just like when we were in New York, I made sure that everywhere Doug was, I was, because everywhere he was, there was a camera. Barry Bee and Chill Will, the other members of The Get Fresh Crew, accepted my membership in the group. The only resistance came from Trisha, one of the mothers of Doug's children, because she saw my potential. She always had a comment about my weight. My weight was my weakest link, and for her to continually point that out was her way of exposing my vulnerability.

Ever since I saw a woman in the bed of Doug's apartment suite, I thought about him, even though I knew he was a man I could never be with. Doug had two baby mothers, whose infants were born months apart. And now he was in bed with a third woman, while the other two fought over him. Yet alone in my suite, Doug dominated my thoughts, even while Bryant phoned constantly from New York. I complained to Bryant, "Doug is fucking with my money. I still haven't gotten paid."

Like every woman—from Shawna, the stylist who would go out of her way to buy me jacked-up clothes, to regular groupies throwing themselves at him—I wanted to get my claws into Doug, to devour him. Trying to sleep one night, as I tossed and turned I decided, *I'm not gonna sell the sex, 'cause that ain't gonna work for me. I'm just gonna get him to open up to me, so I can learn more than those bitches ever could.*

Doug phoned me one night after he had gotten rid of one of his chicks. I grabbed my nail kit because I had the idea that by giving Doug a manicure, we could quickly form an intimacy through gentle touch, conversation, and quiet laughter. Without flaunting my sexuality, I could be close to Doug in a way that distinguished me from the groupies who craved his attention. I knew that the manicures would become a bridge to become closer to him. During these interludes, Doug exposed his vulnerabilities, his dreams, and he gradually came to trust me—I wanted that. We admired our mutual knowledge of R&B. Doug would prepare veggie burgers and avocado salads for me. Together we listened to his music, and he would be shocked that I had memorized his lyrics. He would rhyme, and I would sing with him: A simple manicure had done the trick.

As the days turned into weeks, I continuously asked Doug about my expense money. "I'm waiting for the label!" he would reply.

"Here I am opening up and telling you about my situation and you're making me jump through hoops to get my money. You got money. Give me mine. Even if it means fronting me the money until the label pays you back." Not getting any answers that made sense, I kept nagging Doug, because I needed my money.

Bryant was back in New York, giving me grief, complaining about how long I had been away. While Bryant and I no longer had a physical relationship, emotionally there was still a bond. Doug's entourage suspected that there was something going on between Doug and me, although that wasn't true. Perhaps it was because I no longer held him in awe. Together we would get caught up in moments. In front of whomever was in the room, I would dance close to him and he wouldn't move away. The opinions of others were of no concern to me. My desire was to stay as close to Doug E. as I could.

The process to develop my wardrobe for the stage should have been easier than it was. But Shawna was threatened by the closeness between Doug and me. Knowing her from New York, I never felt that she could be a sister friend. And my instincts proved right, as Shawna continuously bought ill-fitting outfits for me, until she was eventually fired.

Doug continued to make it clear that he was serious about me losing weight. "Tarsha must report to the gym every single day," he announced in front of the group. Since I was the only woman in The Get Fresh Crew, I felt far greater pressure to drop the pounds. I resented that men weren't made to feel as conscious about their weight as women. Chill Will would entice me into eating junk food and then tattle to Doug when I succumbed to the giant ice-cream cones, beef link sausages, and dinner rolls he dangled in my face.

Though we constantly flirted, when it came to business, Doug was a taskmaster. One day, he paid an unannounced visit to my suite like a military reconnaissance team. He strode past me and walked straight to my refrigerator. From his bent-over posture, it was obvious that what he saw dealt a powerful body blow. The longer he was silent, the more uncomfortable I felt. When he gathered his words, he broke me down. "So you were really gonna lose the weight, huh? Nah, you're not serious. You ain't focused. You see En Vogue? Do you see their bodies? Do you see them carrying weight and eating all kinds of crap? Do you know how many people would love to be in your shoes? Nah, you ain't serious! This ain't gonna work out!"

My eyes never lifted from the floor as I pleaded, "All right, I'm going to, but I can't just stop eating! And where you have us living, you can't get no healthy food. And besides, I don't know what's healthy and what's not." Even though I babbled on, there was nothing I could say to justify my lack of discipline. The big break that I had dreamed of, working with one of the most successful artists in hip-hop, was slipping through my fingers. Crying, I ran to Chill Will, whining that losing the weight wasn't easy. But even through my tears, I knew I had to suck it up and show Doug that I was serious about being a member of The Get Fresh Crew.

I went on a ten-day water-only fast. It continued through the hot, twice-per-day grueling rehearsals, fittings and studio work. Again, I asked Doug about my money, and still was given the same bullshit answer. Finally I called Bust It Records to find out where the fuck my money was. The accounting department said that the check was sent to Doug. "We gave it to him. All of your money was included with Doug's money." I was heated and went to see Doug. Everybody from the choreographer to Trisha, his baby's mother, was waiting to talk to him, and so was I. Doug noticed me and handed me a check.

I took one glance at it. "This isn't all of the money I'm owed."

"What are you talking about? That's all of the money," he replied.

"This is not all of the money I'm owed."

"This is all of money I owe you. The rest you gotta get from the label."

"Well, that's bullshit, 'cause that label said they put my money in your check."

"No, they did not cut it in my check. I don't know what they told you that for . . . but the money they cut in my check is my money."

Beyond heated, I returned to New York without being paid and with a kidney so fucked up from the weight loss that I was admitted to Astoria General. Bryant rushed home from Syracuse to take me to the hospital, where I remained with an IV for five days. Though I repeatedly called Doug, he couldn't be located. It took three days for him to be notified. Even then, Doug and I didn't see each other for three weeks. There were no flowers, no phone calls, no visits. Nobody from The Get Fresh Crew, including Doug, came to visit me in the hospital or when I went home, even when they promised that they would. Even though Bryant was the attentive boyfriend, I still felt extremely hurt, and furious. Here I was stuck in bed because of Doug and that water fast. My kidneys almost shut down, and I thought, *I went to LA with those niggas, got sick and they don't care.* And when it was clear that Doug occupied my thoughts and had some influence over me, Bryant's jaws became tight.

Finally Doug resurfaced, and when I heard his voice, all was forgiven and my anger evaporated. Bryant was not so forgiving, frowning whenever he knew Doug was on the telephone. Weight continued to fall off of me, until I was slim and trim. My gay godbrother showed me how to dress to accentuate my new physique and how to wear lip gloss, and gave me a dope weave. The sneakers and cover-up clothes–wearing Tarsha was dead and gone, without a memorial service.

When I finally drove up to Harlem, one month later, and Doug saw the brand-new me emerge all fly from the car, his expression changed from nonchalance to lust. "So now we're ready to do business," he said, smiling and rubbing his hands.

This time, when I moved, he moved.

SEVEN

HIT OF WONDERS

Jonesy's Juice:

Russell Simmons: "Good morning, Russell" is all you need to say before he launches into a blistering ten-minute promotion of twenty-six products he's created in the last two days. No need to ask him any questions, just hang on, go along for the ride, until you remember it's your radio show that he's almost hijacked.

Russell and I met about ten years ago in the Hamptons at Andre Harrell's birthday party. Since I know how to pitch too, I told him how fabulous my website, missjones.net, was. Intrigued, he said he would phone to make an offer to acquire the gossip department on my site to merge with his now-defunct 360hiphop.com. Sure enough, Russell was true to his word, and he had a big check cut for me by the following Friday. Russell has been consistent in giving a break to young, up-and-coming talents. He had wanted to sign me to a record contract with Def Jam, but I chose to go with Andre Harrell. In hindsight, Russell would've been the better bet. God bless you and good night.

"**J**ust flow with it. You're putting too much concentration on it. Just flow. You'll be fine," Doug would say, as he shaved intently in his hotel bathroom mirror. The Get Fresh Crew rehearsed at the hotel, in restaurants, and during airport layovers. I can't remember trying to catch a flight without sprinting through the airport. Sometimes Doug would use his influence to have the airline agent phone the gate and ask them to hold the plane while he signed autographs. One time they brought the motherfuckin' plane back. Doug's beat box went a long way. Those were different times. Late 1991.

"THIS IS CALLED THE SHOW...AH AH AH AH... BUKA BUKA BUKA. MISS JONES...MISS JONES." Doug would beat box my introduction under my vocal rendition of Denise Williams's song "There's Nothing Better That I Want to Do." Audiences responded to me with curiosity, then enthusiasm. Here I was, the only female member of an all-male group, so it was expected that I stood out beyond being just another pretty face. After I completed my solo, I would glance at Chill Will, who shrugged as I moonwalked to the rear of the stage. Because there were no formal rehearsals, every show with Doug was different. The group members knew from his glance what direction he was going to take the performance. You had to be in position to come onstage, and know your song cues.

"Look, I got to get to class. Call me tomorrow," Bryant would brush me off when I phoned to share my excitement. He would act as though he was missing out on my good fortune while he completed his courses at Syracuse University. In order to mask his jealousy, he would say, "This girl in my class has been checking me out. And she looks good to me too." It became normal for him to behave disinterested or try to make me feel bad when I touched base with him. And the more he behaved that way, the more I would confide in Doug and ask for his guidance. Nothing at all romantic. Doug continued to receive my manicures and in return I got great conversation from someone who genuinely acted like they cared. Doug was an excellent sounding board. He was forced to grow up fast, because he'd been in the industry since he was very young. He'd seen the jealous boyfriends and girlfriends come and go.

Doug's tightness with money made me not like him sometimes. Fighting over a damn $35 per diem. In some ways Doug was generous to a fault, but for little shit you always had to fight for life. For a nickel-and-dime check. When you stepped to Doug about it, he had a way of talking to you that made you feel your beef wasn't a big deal or it was really your fault. My money came from the $35 per diems and television-appearance fees received from the AFTRA union.

City after city became an exciting blur. California, North Carolina, Virginia and throughout the South and the Midwest was on-the-job training for me, with appearances on BET's Rap City and House of Blues, among others. Rapper MC Hammer had us living near his luxurious compound in Fremont, California, for months and working out in his gym. Hammer's 40,000 square-foot house had Italian marble floors, a bowling alley, a recording studio, a thirty-three-seat theater, two swimming pools, tennis courts, a baseball diamond and a seventeen-car garage. When I returned home, I would drive to Syracuse to spend some time trying to reconnect romantically with Bryant before The Get Fresh Crew would hit the road again, often for weeks, even months at a time. I could already see that Bryant didn't understand the demands the industry made on me. He felt he wasn't getting the same time from me that he had before. And he was correct. Our time together was tense, distant, and though I was there to spend time with him, he was often either in class, working, or just plain gone. And then the telephone would ring and I was back on the road.

"We just got called to do *Soul Train*," I reluctantly told Bryant after arriving at the Syracuse apartment. The Get Fresh Crew had literally arrived home that morning, and I immediately drove to attend Bryant's college graduation the next day. As soon as I had set my luggage down in the living room, Doug's assistant called to say, "Doug needs you in

New York, 'cause you all have been asked to do *Soul Train*. Y'all have to leave for California in the morning."

"And what did you tell them?" Bryant asked.

"I didn't tell them anything other than I want to do the show."

"I was there for your graduation. Your mother was not at yours, and I can't believe that you aren't gonna be there for me!" Bryant was disappointed and furious. He couldn't accept that as much as I wanted to support him, I wasn't going to turn my back on the chance to perform on *Soul Train*. I had come too far to blow it now. Bryant threw in my face that he was there when my mother died. He accused me of never being supportive of him, and hurled accusations that I was a selfish bitch. He used every word he could think of to cause me pain, until I had to respond. The more the argument continued, the uglier the words became.

"Had you graduated on time, I could've been there for you, so don't get mad at me just 'cause you messed around and chose to hang out all of the time."

If it wasn't becoming clear to Bryant, it was crystal clear to me that he and I were leading completely different lives. Neither one of us wanted to openly acknowledge the chasm as wide as the Grand Canyon that had wedged between us. Bryant saw the control that Doug had over me as I tossed my luggage in the trunk of the car. He began to hate the man that was receiving so much of my attention, especially on the eve of his college graduation.

During the scorching summer of 1992, Doug, Barry Bee, Chill Will, and I would create new music nearly every night at Barry Bee's house. Often we didn't begin until midnight, waiting around for Doug to appear. The creative atmosphere was nurturing. I would sing off-key and make musical mistakes, and Doug still embraced me. He allowed me the creative freedom to find my voice and to explore new melodies. Though Doug wasn't a professional singer, he knew the vocal instrument and could create a song out of thin air. Barry Bee would make a beat and then grab an old-school record and steal a horn from it. Then he would spin another record and steal a bass from it. Now he had a bass, a horn and the beat. Doug and I would write a rap, and Barry Bee would loop the beat.

Bryant would insist on staying for the sessions with me. Though I appreciated that he was trying to be both territorial and a supportive boyfriend, it was uncomfortable with him sitting twiddling his thumbs. I felt as though I had to rush the work because he had to be at his job at the paint factory early in the morning. Eventually, Bryant stopped coming because Doug could sense Bryant's impatience and felt that Bryant was stifling his creativity. Since they had no relationship, Doug didn't trust Bryant and didn't want his raps lifted. Doug told me, "I understand he wants to make sure that you get home safe, but we need to mesh as a group."

Doug started taking me home. We would exchange intimate details about our respective relationships. According to Doug, he wasn't involved with either of his baby mommas. He lived apart from them in his own Harlem brownstone. Doug wanted to make sure that his children knew each other and wanted to have amicable relationships with both women.

Months earlier, during my first trip to Los Angeles, when Hammurabi Bey, Doug's dad, thought that there was something going on, Barry Bee and Chill Will didn't—they *knew* what was unfolding in front of their own eyes. "All right, it's all fun and games until you got a fist in your mouth, coming in at five in the morning with your lipstick smudged," Chill Will, the cutup, would joke, if he would enter a room and witness Doug and me in an innocent, yet awkward moment. Though Doug and I were absolutely, positively not physically involved, if Bryant had seen us lying next to each other watching a video, he would not have been happy. Doug laughed when Chill Will made his snide comments. So did I. Barry Bee and Chill Will were the only two people we felt comfortable being openly affectionate around. Long after Barry Bee and Chill Will were snoring at their apartments,

Doug and I often sat in his red Jeep Cherokee talking about everything. But as much as we talked, Doug and I danced around the heavy tension that kept us connected.

One torrential rainy morning, around 4:00 A.M., Doug and I were still talking in his Jeep outside of Barry Bee's building, not wanting to part after the recording session. But this time, there were heavy gulfs of silences between our words. Doug dodged my flirtation, restraining his body as though he was unsure as to what to do with my affection, and unclear if I was playing around or chasing him for real. The reality was that I chased Doug out of my own loneliness. I lived with Bryant, and he was officially my boyfriend, but the pain of living with someone who had no understanding of my new life was more than I could bear. I didn't possess the level of maturity at that time to have a heart-to-heart with Bryant. Instead I sought what I needed outside the relationship, in an emotional affair with Doug.

When Doug finally gave in and kissed me inside his Jeep, during the wee hours of the morning, our passion was the fulfillment of a premeditated fantasy. Doug and I admitted that for months we had dreamed of that moment. By the time we finally came up for air, the rain had slowed to a trickle, and there was a relief, which we both welcomed and despised. We knew that because of our mutual entanglements, that restrictive line that kept us apart had not moved one inch.

Doug continued to perform on solo tours around the world; I worked on my music and often performed one-woman showcases around New York City. While he was away, Doug phoned me from wherever, and we would talk until the sun rose or until it set. Though I was physically attracted to him, our relationship was instead deeply emotional, as I still sought assurance and advice from him about my career and Bryant.

Bryant had lost his control over me. Here was his woman leaving the bed in the middle of the night to whisper through a prolonged international telephone conversation with a famous entertainer. In his powerlessness, Bryant would come into the kitchen. "Get off of the fucking phone! Fucking disrespectful bitch," he would yell, wanting Doug to hear him, snatching and hanging up the telephone. In front of my dancers, he would challenge my authority to reprimand them or would talk shit to embarrass me, especially when I was about to be publicly honored. Once while traveling in Washington, D.C., to perform at BET's Sprite Night, I purchased expensive designer sunglasses for Bryant. In the limo, in front of my dancers and road crew, Bryant unexplainedly rolled down the window, broke the sunglasses in pieces and tossed them out, sneering, "That's what I think of these glasses and that's what I think of you." We continued in stunned silence to the hotel.

"You gotta get up here! We gotta write a song tonight; the nigga wants to hear something tomorrow," Ron G, who later became my producer, ordered. The nigga in question was Bill Stephney, president of StepSun Records. Ronald Bowser, aka Ron G, had walked my tape into Bill's office. Bill was pleased with what he heard. "I want to sign her. Y'all got any more songs?" Ron G had lied and said that we did.

That night I drove to the Polo Grounds, where Ron G lived, and wrote "Where I Wanna Be Boy." I recorded the lead and background vocals on ancient equipment that required you to sing the whole song over again if you made a mistake. At that time, we didn't have digital studio equipment. But I sang my heart out, determined that this was going to be my opportunity to get a record deal.

StepSun Records was not my first choice in record labels, but I was hungry and they were the only ones biting at the time. Doug advised me to sit back and wait, but I figured any opportunity to be seen was better than waiting for some money. I signed with StepSun for a measly $50,000, but fortunately, beyond the money issue, my gamble paid off.

In 1994, when my first single "Where I Wanna Be Boy" cracked the Billboard Top 100 chart, industry heavyweights like Russell Simmons and Andre Harrell took notice. Tommy Boy Music, which Bill Stephney had contracted to distribute his records, stepped in as the distributor, because Bill didn't have the manpower to turn that song and my career into revenue for StepSun. Tommy Boy sent in their staff, radio people, publicists, and marketing people, and in effect shut Bill down. It was due to Tommy Boy's push that I achieved the visibility from appearances on television shows such as *Soul Train* and BET's *Rap City.*

During my recovery from surgery to remove a tumor that had returned in my jaw, I read Mary J. Blige's album-liner notes and learned who was guiding her career. If Mary and I had grown up in the same housing project, she may have been one of those rough girls I would have run from, or we may have been good friends. Doug was on the road down South with his new artist, Lil' Vicious. Two artist managers had discovered Mary J. Blige, and though I felt embarrassed because I looked homely with my mouth full of braces, I put ego aside and took a meeting with them. What was a promising start, where I felt I was in the hands of professionals who could maximize my budding exposure, soon became another problem that I had to handle. During a supportive moment, Bryant organized my receipts and accounting records and discovered that some money was missing. The check had been transferred to an accountant, who one of the managers had hired. He then got an advance against the check without notifying me. When I confronted him, he lied to my face. I reminded him that from the beginning of our relationship all monies were to be given to me and then I would pay him his commission. Not vice versa. For the next few months, they essentially became my gofers; because the trust was gone and our relationship never recovered.

Eventually, the managers and the accountant were fired. And that was the first and last time I allowed anyone to be in charge of my finances.

Doug returned from performing in Europe. Though we had kept in touch on the telephone, I'd really missed seeing him. And unbeknownst to him, I had continued to lose weight, due to a liquid diet, and had totally revamped my image. At my show at the Puck Building, Doug was so pleased that his protégé had come into her own. I was thin but healthy and wore a red DKNY tennis skirt and white top, with a Shirley Temple ponytail—my trademark look. When Doug hugged me backstage after the show, the uncertainty that I had seen in his eyes when we had first kissed disappeared. I knew in my heart that he wanted to go to the next level with me.

Members of the media and those around us inquired and wanted to know the scope of our relationship, yet we still kept it private. When asked by a reporter, I would reply, "Just because I'm a girl and he's a guy means nothing."

Bryant and I continued to drift apart. Both of us refused to acknowledge that the bond we had overcome so much turmoil to achieve was slipping away. He'd always wanted me to be a star, but he'd never thought it would happen. Neither he nor I understood the realities of the entertainment business. The frequent travel. The constant rehearsals. The media, who ignored a star's significant other. Though the rewards were great, the challenges to an already fragile relationship were insurmountable. Depending on his mood, Bryant would be happy for me one day and aloof the next. Breaking up was never an option— as my mother always said, "You never leave, no matter how bad it gets." In my mind, if we were going to break up, it wasn't going to be because of my unconsummated relationship with Doug. And Doug knew we wouldn't make love until we'd both ended our relationships.

Rashaad Burton Smith and Samuel Avon Marshall, aka Tumblin' Dice, were one of the hottest production teams. Rashaad handled the beats; Avon was on the keyboards. Doug used his gift of gab and persuaded them to work with me. We would work alternately in Rashaad's Brooklyn apartment, Platinum Island Studios in Manhattan and Studio A in Long Island. Rashaad paid for all of the studio costs and got reimbursed by StepSun for the recording costs.

There had been a knock at the door of one of the booths at Studio A as I was laying down the vocals for "Don't Front." When I opened the door, there stood a tall, muscular, dread-locked brother with a gruff voice. He'd clearly had a beef when he knocked on the door, but changed his direction as his eyes rolled over my body.

"Oh! That's a hot little song. Who produced for you?" It was hip-hop superstar Busta Rhymes. I had heard of him from Leaders of the New School, but we had never met. Rashaad had been producing Busta on his upcoming solo album, *The Coming*.

"Rashaad produced it for me," I replied, looking down the hallway for Rashaad.

"Oh, that's my man. Where he at?"

"He's outside. I think."

Moments later, through the recording studio window, I saw an an-imated Busta up in Rashaad's face, the volume of their voices seeping through the window. From what I saw, it was better that I stayed where I was. When I asked Rashaad about their conversation, he said, "The nigga mad 'cause this 'Don't Front' track was originally his. But he didn't pay me for it. Stephney wanted it for you and came with the paper, so I explained to that nigga that I had to move on the track."

Later, I found Busta in another studio. "If you still want the song, you can have it, 'cause I don't want any problems, especially in the be-ginning of my career."

"No, that's between me and that nigga Rashaad. If anything, maybe you and Rampage could do a remix together after the song blows, but you sound real good."

Busta was attracted to me. It was written all over his grinning face. The attraction was mutual. We exchanged telephone numbers and talked about me doing vocals on his album. Over the next week, Busta and I arranged to meet at Backspin Studios, where he was producing a solo album for Rampage of Flip Mode Squad fame. There was no denying that there was chemistry between us. He carried himself like a magnificent, brilliant star, confident of his masculine strength, but was able to be gentle with those not possessing his gifts. When he explained something as simple as how he wanted me to break down a song, it was as if he were giving instruction on how he wanted me to respond to his lovemaking. Our eyes would linger, our voices would whisper and we would giggle at absolutely nothing.

Under the initial guise of our love for hip-hop and R&B, Busta would phone me right after Bryant left for work, and then we would speak at least three or four times every day. He was curious about my family, my goals, and my needs, and cared so much that he actually remembered the information. He made it clear that he and his crazy, as he called his baby's mother, were not a couple. Busta's recognizable truck became a frequent landmark outside my Astoria apartment. Busta incorrectly thought that if he slumped down in the driver's seat, no one would recognize him. As soon as my friends saw his truck park in front of my building, they would do a special whistle up to my window to signal that Busta was downstairs.

As our fondness grew for each other, Busta would sneak me off to one of his many apartments from Flatbush to Long Island. On one occasion, we hung out at his mother's house. After introducing us, Busta guided me upstairs to his bedroom, where we lounged on his bed, watching the latest videos and snacking on junk food. During a quiet moment, Busta leaned over to kiss me. Though I was beginning to feel comfortable with him, I moved away. "We don't have to do nothing. That's not why I brought you here," he reassured. Now thinking he was a gentleman, I fought the temptation to wrap my arms around him. I was tempted to, but I didn't.

Busta would book me for various studio sessions. Everything was professional and aboveboard, until he came into the recording booth. From the closeness of our bodies, our physical chemistry, I knew we were on the fast track to some serious bone-jumping. One night our impulse to fast track to his apartment was derailed when I learned that

my car had been towed. It was then I realized that Busta was struggling to launch his career and didn't have any money. I lent him money
to rent cars or take care of other expenses. Then there were rumors
that Leaders of the New School were breaking up and no one knew
who was going to end up where. As time went on, I saw more of his financial roller coaster than I cared to. Busta never remembered that
small gesture, a gesture that he needed at that time. He was always out
for whatever would make his situation hotter. He wouldn't support
those who were not on the hot list. Busta would scold his protégé members of the Flip Mode Squad when they would complain about not getting paid for their work. "Y'all are nothing but bills! I don't need none
of y'all! Instead of bitching, y'all need to start selling records and writing hotter shit!" Somehow both Doug and Busta liked to talk you out
of your rightfully earned money.

With my car at the pound, Busta paid me in advance for the studio
session. But the chivalry ended there. Although we had been flirting all
up in each other's grill, I knew that Busta was not my man; at least not
in the way I wanted a man to be. Still I needed him to court me—to
show me he knew how to be a gentleman. As a result, I assumed that
he would not deduct the $150 advance I paid for the tow pound. But
when my studio paycheck arrived reflecting the docked money, my
fantasy just laughed in my face.

It became evident that Bill Stephney was not an effective
manager. StepSun Records was squandering opportunities
to advance my career. Plus, he would dog singers like Mary J. Blige
and Zhané, saying, "They aren't that talented. Besides, do you think
that another 'Hey Mr. DJ' song is going to blow up?" And as I should
have expected, Bill's criticism soon rained down on me. "Well, if you
wrote songs like Mary J., maybe you would sell records like her."

Katie Jones, executive producer of *Soul Train* continues to be a take-
charge producer who always finds a way to solve a problem. Back then,
she saw that StepSun lacked the budget and the vision to promote me

aggressively. Even though she did not personally benefit by doing so, she supported me beyond the call of duty and booked me as a solo artist three times, which she had never done for an artist before. During one taping, I needed a guy to lip-synch onstage, so Katie suggested that Bryant fill in. Bryant learned the timing backstage in ten minutes, and the appearance was a great success. I will always have the deepest appreciation for Katie for putting the pressure on StepSun to promote my music.

When I returned to New York, Chill Will and I were hanging out at Barry Bee's apartment, when Chill Will blurted out the news. As close as he and I were, he was naive as to how deeply I felt about Doug, so he would just tell me shit, and then go back to remixing a tape. But this time, the news cut through me like a meteor landing in the desert.

Doug had impregnated both of his baby's mothers—again.

Chill Will brought it. And I played it off like I already knew. But the news hit me so hard, my feet couldn't wait to find an excuse to leave and confront Doug. The muthafucka had been lying all along. They were pregnant, at the same time. Doug and I had talked about our plans to be together. But he had never intended that that day would ever come.

"**W**hy didn't you tell me that Gigi and Trisha are pregnant?"

"Who told you? I wanted to tell you myself."

"When?"

"When the time was right." That was how Doug deflected all of his bullshit. Any time he was backed into a corner, his excuse for being there was because the timing wasn't right. I cried tears enough to drown in. But I never gave Doug the satisfaction of witnessing my pain. After all, I had no right to confront him. From the beginning, both of us had known what we were getting into. It made no sense for me to act like a character from *One Life to Live*. I had partnered with Doug in creating the drama we were both facing. Still, I was devastated by Doug's new embryos, and Busta was a perfect place to re-bound.

Busta and I continued to hang out everywhere, using the music as an excuse to get together. For me, Busta was a loud, rebellious, and intoxicating scoundrel, whom I was thoroughly charmed by. In his presence, I canceled the rule that I held out to Doug—of not sleeping with a man who wasn't committed to me. The music Busta created was rugged and sexy and befitting of true superstar royalty. And he made himself accessible to me. Whenever I wanted to hear or see him, Busta was there. Unlike Doug, who was so busy running between his career, his babies' mothers ... and a wannabe born-again Christian who liked to get finger-fucked.

Doug and I still spoke on the telephone, pretending that we could maintain a friendship. He was aware that Busta and I had hooked up, and he knew there wasn't a damn thing he could do about it. Privately, I felt about Doug: *Hey, you're still in deep with your baby mommas, which means you don't care about me. I'm not gonna stop living. My emotional needs still have to be met. I deserve to have a man I can trust, even when he is nowhere around.*

Busta made it clear that I was the woman and he was the man. He dominated and you succumbed by following his lead. Our relationship was physically consummated in a room he rented on Flatbush Avenue, in Brooklyn, New York. Though I didn't like kissing him because he smoked cigarettes, our lovemaking was electric and passionate. Busta was as gentle as he could be, because he was packing. Busta's lovemaking was not for the timid or faint of heart. The fact that our lovemaking never lasted too long didn't bother me, because I didn't enjoy his drops of sweat raining down on me. What did annoy me was that the after-sessions were seriously lacking.

When we emerged from the tiny bedroom, water bugs and roaches scattered everywhere. Ignoring our multilegged guests, Busta would stroll around the apartment butt-naked, then shower and go into the kitchen and fry an egg sandwich—for himself. I guess I should be grateful. It's not like he didn't offer me a bite.

Busta's lovemaking prowess reflected in his daily life. He has always been an opportunist, looking out for Busta. He may offer you a bite, but only after he had eaten most of the meal. Once I put him in a reality box, I knew I could still love him, as long as I had no expectations beyond who he truly was.

In 1995, life was great. My newfound celebrity made it easy. I no longer had to stand on line to enter a club; invitations to the best parties came pouring in. The road tour promoting "Where I Wanna Be Boy" was very successful, resulting in a spike in sales. I appeared on BET's Sprite Night and presented at the Soul Train Music Awards. My video had hit the airwaves, featuring Doug wrapping his coat around me. And when we weren't fighting, Bryant functioned as my road manager.

Busta and I continued to sex each other and exchanged words of love. But he became terrified of people finding out about our affair. I trusted his judgment. It made me feel like he was looking out for our best interests and that he knew more about the pitfalls of the industry than I. We played cat and mouse, sneaking and hiding. If we were going to an industry party, Busta would warn, "Don't act like we're together. Don't act like there is anything going on! You don't want people in the industry in your business." In public, aside from a twinkle in his eye or a two-way message to meet him outside, he treated me like I was just another colleague.

Busta would invite me on his national road trips, but I always refused because I could never trust how he would act in public. I was determined never to be the one isolated in some lonely hotel room waiting for the superstar to arrive, my sole contact being one of his loyal lackeys. So I chose to keep our tryst local.

In spite of his paranoia, while lying in bed at my Madison Avenue apartment the night before HOT 97's Summer Jam, Busta proposed marriage. According to Busta, he had mad love for me and wanted me to become his wife.

"Are you serious?" I asked. Busta smiled and nodded.

"**Yes,**" I answered. I floated on air and was pleased that Busta wanted to spend his life with me. At the same time, I wasn't prepared to rent a catering hall or design wedding invitations. I just loved that Busta Rhymes had proposed. And that our relationship would move to whatever the next level was. I never considered what marriage meant. I really needed to see more of who he was. During a meeting at a music publishing house, I excitedly spread the news of the proposal, without mentioning Busta's name, to a roomful of strangers. I then flew down to L'Impasse, a Greenwich Village upscale boutique. There I purchased the most beautiful lilac-colored, semi-low-cut summer gown to wear to the Summer Jam concert.

When I arrived at Busta's dressing room, there was all that I needed to see. I knocked. Busta answered, "Wassup?" Busta and a frying-pan-faced girl stared at me like I was Mike Wallace from *60 Minutes*. It was obvious that the girl didn't know who I was, but Busta joined her in the charade. Since I decided not to cause a scene, especially in my fancy L'Impasse dress, I covered for Busta, asking, "Can I use your bathroom?"

I was furious. Here I was all dressed up in my celebratory engagement dress and my so-called fiancé had suddenly come down with a terminal case of amnesia. Mumbling nothing in particular, I left Busta's dressing room, slamming the door. The remainder of the evening, including the concert starring Jay-Z, DMX, Redman, Method Man, Ruff Ryders, Ja Rule, 702, and the Violator crew—Busta Rhymes, Missy Elliott, and Q-Tip—remain a blur. When Busta blew up my telephone and I finally decided to answer, he offered a bullshit explanation: "You know I couldn't say nothin' with her there!"

"First of all, you say 'her' like I'm supposed to know who this bitch is. There was no thought of her when you were asking me to be your wife." Soon I believed the lies that Busta was telling me. That the girl was a nobody, that I was the woman he wanted to be with.

One morning, like clockwork, Busta phoned me. Answering, I was glad that he called, until I heard an angry female voice in his background. It became apparent by what she was saying that Busta's baby's mother had walked in on him, and he tried to play it off by yelling at me, "I told you not to call here!"

"What are you talking about, Busta?" I couldn't believe that he would try to play me out like that. Like Doug, he had made it seem like he and his baby's mother had no relationship. And like Doug, Busta had lied.

I had never considered leaving Bryant for Busta. Mainly, Busta's total focus was his career and himself. If that meant that I had to be thrown to wolves to advance or protect himself, then I would be the one tossed. When I compared Bryant with Busta, as tumultuous as our relationship was, Bryant provided me with a level of stability that I never had with Busta. Busta's so-called proposal had been a game to get in deeper with me. It was his lame attempt to get me to do freaky things with him sexually. Busta knew the type of girl I was—the type of shit I would take and what I would not. So he never asked me outright to do freaky shit, because he knew that I would blow up his spot. Thus he had to play a mind game and come at me in a straight-laced way—with a marriage proposal.

With Busta, it was only sex. And I never trusted him with my emotions. And never will. So the relationship had its limits. I learned not to trust a proposal of marriage made in bed.

Former NFL New York Giant running back Rodney Hampton nagged Shawna, Doug's former stylist, to introduce us after he had spotted me at an industry after-party. When it was clear that Rodney wanted to be more than friends, I told him the truth:

"Look, there is so much intricate shit going on with me. You think I'm madly in love with Bryant, but you don't even know half the shit I'm dealing with."

Rodney later told me, "I always thought you and I would get together, because we never messed it up with a physical relationship. I'm glad we're friends." Rodney, true to his word, became a supportive friend, ultimately buying me a brand-new Altima when I needed a car. When I drove home in the brand-new Altima, Bryant's lips were poked out at first, but I was like, "Look, I'm not fucking Rodney, and if the nigga want to get me a car and this is something we both can use, then what are you mad about?" Bryant quickly overcame his ego and wanted to sport around town in the car the very next day. He became seduced by and yet often despised the perks that I began to receive from my rising profile.

EIGHT

TONGUES WAGGING

Jonesy's Juice:

Wendy: "Jonesy! It's Wendy. Don't talk. Just listen. I am so concerned about you. Fuck all of this radio shit because at the end of the day, we are women in radio in the struggle. And mothers. I am just concerned about your surgery. . . . Is it the same surgery you had years ago? How are you, Jonesy? What's going on? Talk to me."

To this day, I still remember her husky baritone whisper on the other end of my telephone as she hid her conversation from her husband.

She's so dramatic. And transparent.

She was hoping I would confirm the lies that I had had gastric surgery.

"No, Wendy. It's some serious health shit."

"Well, don't you worry 'cause Egypt [Power 105.1] is still unlistenable. . . . She could be gone for a year and nobody would notice. . . . Call me whenever you need me."

Two weeks later, Wendy says on air, ". . . the only television camera that Jonesy needs to be in front of is VH1's *Celebrity Fit Club*."

After all of her years in radio, Wendy Williams has not elevated above curb level in terms of paving the way for other women in radio.

Disappointing.

"**M**iss Jones is some broke-down, buck-tooth bitch," the column in the ghetto rag *Round Da Way Connections* read in 1995, when a press release announcing my upcoming album circulated. And the bullshit was signed "Buc Wild." The alleged Buc Wild was supposed to be a fifteen-year-old named Timothy. I later found out that a grown man had been impersonating his little half brother Timothy for years.

Damn.

That's like a parent ruining their three-year-old child's credit.

I was pissed. Especially when Wendy Williams, who was at HOT 97 at that time, would give the rag a shout out.

"Who da fuck is dis nigga Buc Wild?" Bryant asked.

At that time, there was a locally known rapper named Buckwild, and we thought it was him and called to get with the brother. Bryant was told, "Wrong dude. That definitely ain't me." Bryant finally got the right telephone number to the rag, before using the paper to collect pigeon droppings from our window ledge.

My bad to the Astoria Projects' pigeons. Your droppings deserved VIBE *at least.*

Bryant wasn't no gangsta when he got this Buc Wild person on the telephone: "I'm calling about this statement written about Miss Jo—"

"Yeah, what about it?"

"I'm her man and I don't appreciate—"

"Yeah, I wrote it! What the fuck do you wanna do? Youse a bitch ass too, nigga!" And the punk slammed down the telephone.

Bryant was heated. And so was I. But I didn't want him to go to the rag's offices, 'cause that would only make this Buc Wild person write more crap. Frankly, Bryant wasn't trying to get out the door to do the "defend my woman" thang. Not out of some "turn da other cheek" Ghandi passivity, but 'cause nobody knew what this Buc Wild person looked like. Or if his telephone swagga had any street cred.

My first day of
kindergarten.

PHOTO: COURTESY OF
TARSHA JONES

I swear, I think
my dad wanted
a son. This is
one of the many
hats Sonny
bought me.

PHOTO: COURTESY OF
TARSHA JONES

Easter. Age 6 inside the
foyer of our apartment in
the Astoria Projects.

PHOTO: COURTESY OF TARSHA JONES

My sisters, Marcia, 13 years old, and Audrey, 14 years old, one Easter in our apartment.

PHOTO: COURTESY OF TARSHA JONES

Marcia, me, my mom, and Audrey in 1985. No weaves; our real hair, bitches!

PHOTO: COURTESY OF TARSHA JONES

Mom and Dad at one of Aunt Nina's dinner parties.

PHOTO: COURTESY OF TARSHA JONES

My biological dad and me on my graduation from junior high school I. S. 126.

PHOTO: COURTESY OF TARSHA JONES

At Aaliyah's album release party shortly before her death in August 2001 in a plane crash. *From left:* Linnie Belcher, Akissa Mendez, and Alia Davis of the R&B group Allure; me; Aaliyah; Charisse Rose of the R&B duo Changing Faces; and Lalisha "Lala" McClean from Allure. PHOTO: RONNIE WRIGHT

Star, Ike Turner, and me after a *Morning Show* interview on Hot 97.

PHOTO: COURTESY OF TARSHA JONES

Me and Diana Ross after a *Morning Show* interview on Hot 97.

PHOTO: COURTESY OF TARSHA JONES

Magic Johnson and me after a *Morning Show* interview on Hot 97.

PHOTO: COURTESY OF TARSHA JONES

LL Cool J and me after a *Morning Show* interview on Hot 97.

PHOTO: COURTESY OF TARSHA JONES

Craig Mac and me after a *Morning Show* interview on Hot 97.

PHOTO: COURTESY OF TARSHA JONES

Hard at work at the station.

PHOTO: COURTESY OF TARSHA JONES

With Tyrese, who sang for me at my 30th birthday party. Fat Man Scoop also performed.

PHOTO: RONNIE WRIGHT

Here I am posing with LL Cool J at the 2000 Online Hip-Hop Awards.

PHOTO: RON GALELLA/WIREIMAGE

Looking good at a promotional party.
PHOTO: RONNIE WRIGHT

Isaac Hayes and I attended the premiere of *Shaft* and weren't we FAB together!

Here I am at my
30th birthday party.

PHOTO: RONNIE WRIGHT

A publicity shot for Hot 97.

Another publicity shot for Hot 97.

Another publicity shot for Hot 97.

PHOTO: DEVONCASS.COM

Have you met
Miss Jones?

PHOTO: DEVONCASS.COM

Shit, nobody was trying to be a corpse in a real-life sequel to a Halloween *movie.*

Buc Wild was not the only one writing shit about me in magazines. But the other stuff was limited to music criticism. One reviewer said I was trying to be another Mary J. Blige. Though it wasn't true, that I could take, because it was never personal. I held on to the hatred of what Buc Wild had scribbled and fantasized about leaving a burning bag of shit on the lawn of his utopia, even though I doubted that he possessed internal peace. But Tupac's rhyme came right on time: "I know you're fed up ladies, but keep your head up." So I kept it movin'. Past the situation and this Buc Wild bastard.

In the January 1996 issue of *The Source* magazine, Buc Wild flipped his opinion for some reason and ass-kissed in his "Reality Check" column: "Ghetto Princess of the Year—missjones (Please forgive me, homegirl. You are definitely where I want to be.)"

What a sorry-assed apology. Who da fuck is he?

Renee of Zhané had a star-studded party at Caliente in Manhattan. Zhané had been featured on Busta's "It's a Party" single, and I looked forward to congratulating her. Busta had squirmed his way back in my life, but our sexual jump-offs were no more than straight-up booty calls. I never trusted him with my emotions, and never will, so the relationship had its limits. Renee's party was just one of the parties I would use to celebrate my birthday week. Greeted by Rodney Hampton, industry well-wishers and friends, I locked eyes with Doug as he sat on the opposite side of the lushly decorated, exclusive nightclub. It was like seeing somebody that you never got over. I didn't know whether to walk toward him or run from the club. I didn't know whether to kiss or hug him. After all, I had my pride, but I didn't want him thinking I had been sitting around waiting for him. With his easy smile, Doug stood to greet me, and it was like time and turmoil had never separated us. The easy comfort and way of being was still there. Doug was my knight in shining armor. At crucial moments, he always appeared out of nowhere. When I was depressed over my mother's death, he opened a new chapter in my life.

"I don't know about you, but not having you in my life the way I used to feels crazy, and I think we need to make a decision to either be together or leave it alone. And not be together the way we had been sneaking, but being together where we tell everybody the truth and we move forward."

And I was like, "What's going to happen to me?" My voice breathed the words. The man who I had adored was reciprocating. Doug was ready and willing to openly share his love with me.

"If you wanna be with me and you wanna be my woman, then it's my job to take care of that. You don't have to worry about what Bryant is going to say, because I'm going to move you out. I'm gonna take care of you. And if you want, we can drive over to your house right now and pack your shit—that's the kind of real nigga I am. And you gotta end shit with Busta." Doug issued this statement with a sense of finality, as if it had been on his mind for a very long time. Zhané's fans were inside Caliente throwing back the flowing champagne. Doug had stopped short of consummating our relationship because he was really struggling with his conscience. He didn't want to hurt the mothers of his children or me. He had said earlier, "I have to slowly pull my head out of the furnace . . . if not, I will be made to suffer."

Doug instructed, "Busta is inside. Now is your chance to tell him." Though I walked with a smile, I nervously approached Busta. Leaning back in his "don't act like you know me" stance, Busta was chilling in a corner, surrounded by his admirers. When he saw me approach he grinned, behaving as if I were a long-lost friend. Tightly gripping his hug, just before he wanted to let go, I whispered, "I'm not gonna be with you anymore. Doug and I are gonna be together now."

Busta stepped back, quickly looking around the club, checking to see if anyone knew what had just transpired. *Miss Jones Dumps Busta Rhymes.* Quickly he gathered himself. "All right. Okay. All right." I gave him a quick peck on the cheek and turned, to see Doug crossing the room toward us.

"Lemme holla at Busta a sec," Doug said, pounding Busta on his shoulder and leading him to a corner draped by red velvet curtains.

Busta spoke first. "Jonesy told me that you and her are going to be together. I wish y'all the best."

Back at the ranch, Bryant continued to live in my apartment, but we led separate lives and shared little common interests and no affection whatsoever. Doug came to my birthday party in Astoria, attracting the entire neighborhood. Though Bryant still lived in my apartment, Doug and I were publicly a couple. Bryant openly cried and became sanctimonious. With all of the shit that I had taken from him for eight years, I could no longer feel for him. For the first time, I felt compassion for myself.

"I understand how you could have done what you did to me with Lisa and them other bitches, because now I'm doing it. I see how easy it was for you."

Without proper representation, my album had not dropped and StepSun Records was folding. After having worked so hard on a labor of love, it was difficult for me to accept that the album wasn't going to be released. To brighten my spirits, Doug bought me a full-length fur coat. He also arranged for me to perform at the then popular Chaz & Wilson's club at Def Jam's promotional listening party. Russell Simmons, LL Cool J, and Mona Scott were there to convince me to sign with Def Jam. Andre Harrell, president of Motown Records, held court at another table. Recording artist Faith was one of the performers. After I had performed a rendition of "Inseparable," the negotiating began between Russell and Andre.

Eventually, I signed with Motown Records. I wasn't going to abandon my man, Doug, and his production company to sign with a different record label. Doug, as a result, was able to create a new imprint with Motown when the label learned that he could attach me.

My lawyer negotiated the $1 million deal. StepSun Records got $250,000 to terminate my contract, and my lawyer and Doug also got a percentage. The rest of the money went toward my recording budget. It was one of the worst business decisions of my life.

The glamorous life came fast and easy. My single "Two Way Street" generated nationwide interview requests and performance dates. After my appearance on Ed Lover and Dr. Dre's popular morning radio show on New York's HOT 97 station to promote my single "Where I Wanna Be Boy," Steve Smith, the general manager of the station, said, "You have a great sound. Have you ever thought of doing radio?" I was flattered, but just played it off like it was no big deal. I was accustomed to people talking loud and saying nothing. Giving you compliments, boasting about their various accomplishments, and meaning none of it. In my mind, Steve was just one more. However, by the time I had reached home late that afternoon, Steve had contacted Motown Records. Unfortunately, they never gave me the message. But Steve, not to be deterred, kept calling, and eventually reached me. He had built HOT 97 by changing the dance format to New York's first rap and hip-hop radio station. HOT 97 was his brainchild, and his relevance to the industry remains unchallenged.

Steve asked me to join Ed Lover and Dr. Dre on their morning show as a cohost. I was ecstatic. Being a cohost on HOT 97 would give me a great opportunity to promote my music career. Had it not been for Ed Lover and Dr. Dre embracing and training me and making me shine, I would not be where I am today. I am eternally grateful to them.

In addition to my duties on the morning show, Steve also offered me a weekend shift. God is truly great. The door opened to an opportunity of a lifetime.

Bryant was furious and probably had been percolating for months. Whenever he paged me I was with Doug, and when I returned home at night, he would order: "Take your fucking clothes off. I want to fuck you." When I resisted, he tore my clothes off, turned the lights off, and forced himself on me. Deep inside, even with my talent and million-dollar deal, I still felt as though I were a piece of meat, ready for consumption by the men in my life. I felt that whatever the man demanded, I had to adhere to his physical and emotional needs, no matter what I truly wanted and needed. My relationship needs always were on a man's back burner. In effect, Bryant's repeated acts were rape, but I never labeled his assault as such. In the Astoria Projects, I'd learned to shut down and let life happen. In my relationships with men, in my world, girls never had the right to demand anything. The warped mind-set was that a man, any man, was better than no man at all. Wherever I was emotionally, regarding my self-esteem and in my relationship with Doug, I still didn't believe that I deserved better. An hour before showtime with Doug and me performing at Manhattan Center, Bryant overheard my telephone conversation reconfirming the schedule. Before every performance, it was my practice to meditate to center myself so I could deliver the best performance possible.

On this night, Bryant had other plans. Ripping off my new blouse and bruising my arm, he yelled, "I fucking bought this shirt. Find something else to wear." Two days later, before my performance with Zhané at Tramps, Bryant decided he would rather fight than drive me to the gig. He did everything he could to purposely sabotage any advancement in my career. This time I stood my ground. I had reached my breaking point. "Get the fuck out, Bryant," I yelled.

"I'm not going no-fucking-where. You leave, bitch."

I left with nothing, leaving behind even my mother's treasured possessions.

When I told Doug, he immediately flew into action. He rented me a high-rise apartment in the West End Towers on Manhattan's west side. And gave instructions to Chill Will to purchase furniture and whatever else I needed, including a $26,000 1996 Elipse convertible. Doug sent me shopping with his American Express credit card and gave me $10,000 to buy whatever I needed, whenever I needed it.

Doug and I waited until he moved me into West End Towers before consummating our relationship. His lovemaking was healing. It had been years since I had been made love to as opposed to being no more than the target of a battering ram. In Doug's arms, I was held as if I was valued—as if I mattered. The fact that we had waited, though tempted often, made the moment all the more special. I was relieved to have a new beginning and turn my back on the past. All that hurt I never wanted to see or feel again. The West End Towers apartment became our haven. Doug never had to arrive with a suitcase, because I purchased boxers, his favorite soaps, fragrance, sneakers, and jeans. His clothes were all neatly folded in his own private dresser. When I knew that he was coming off tour, I prepared his favorite meal: salmon, yucca, artichoke and sun-dried tomatoes and special dressings. He would share with me everything he had experienced while on the road. I would update him on what was happening in my life. Sometimes we would stay at an exclusive Midtown hotel just to get away from the ringing telephone and seclude ourselves from the world. Doug always knew that I was not after his money because I paid for the hotel getaways myself. Due to HBO's taping of Sinbad's Soul Music Festival, the world witnessed our new love as we danced to Evelyn "Champagne" King, Larry Graham & Graham Central Station, and George Clinton under the humid Aruba night sky.

When we returned from Aruba and Doug had left to take business meetings in Los Angeles, Bryant dropped by unannounced, under the guise of wishing me well.

"Hmmm, its aright," Bryant said, as if he was a real estate appraiser. "I could do a whole lot more with this if it were mine though." His comments were stated to try to gauge my reaction. "You ever think about getting back together?"

"No, Bryant."

"How dare you fucking disrespect me?" Bryant unexpectedly punched me so fucking hard that I flew over the sofa like a tossed remote control.

Clutching my face, cowering behind the sofa, I cried, "Get out, Bryant! I'm calling the police!" Bryant seemed startled at his own rage as he slammed out the door.

When I got Doug on the telephone, he was frustrated. "What was he doing there? I'm tired of this shit! I moved you out and he's over there violating!"

"He's hurting. You don't have to worry about him coming back. Plus, now security knows not to let him upstairs."

It was no surprise that Bryant expected me to return to him and the Astoria apartment. After all, I had done so many times before, after years of assault. Although he continued to pay rent, he eventually demolished the apartment to shreds; it took him five years to get his shit together to find his own place to live.

My residency at the West End Towers was eventful. Excitement was always knocking at my door. Once I was startled out of a dream by the frantic buzzing of my intercom. When I answered, sleepy-eyed, I heard a loud commotion before I even said hello. "Who is it?"

"Jonesy, it's Kim!"

"Who?"

"Kim. Can you come downstairs and buzz me in the building?"

It was the rapper Lil' Kim. We had met during a performance at William Patterson University. Doug, Junior M.A.F.I.A., Biggie, and I were on the lineup. Lil' Kim had knocked on the door to my bathroom asking for a place to change clothes. She was not a successful artist at that time. In a business where artists are often competitive instead of supportive, she was so appreciative that I had been real cool to her. Soon we were sharing boyfriend war stories. Lord knows that I was going through my share of it with Doug and his babies' mothers. That first night I told her that I lived in the same building as Biggie and Faith—the West End Towers.

Later we would run into each other a lot at the Sony studios. On one occasion I asked her to listen to my rendition of "Love Under New Management." After, she said, "I never knew you could sing like that." She was wearing a beautiful bracelet that I noticed was damaged and I asked her about it. Without skipping a beat, she said, "Biggie came in and beat me up 'cause he found out that I was fucking around with some nigga."

"But he's married to Faith!" I naively said.

"He don't care! I'm not supposed to do nothin', so he came in here and ripped up my bracelet and left."

Before I could answer Lil' Kim on the intercom, her brother had snatched the telephone, and said, "No, Jonesy! She's drunk. Don't let her in. She's trying to start some shit. And I'm not trying to bail nobody out of jail tonight. I'm not trying to catch no case."

I threw on some shorts and a T-shirt and went downstairs to the security desk. Lil' Kim was screaming. "I went to that bitch's door and she called security to have me removed. Why can't we talk like women?"

Lil' Kim and her crew had been thrown out of the twin tower to my building, in which Biggie Smalls and Faith resided. Seeking another means to force a confrontation with Biggie—Lil' Kim's married lover—and his wife and infant, Lil' Kim wanted me to allow her in so she could go through the underground pass to Biggie and Faith's building. I refused.

Since he was married to Faith, I was surprised that Biggie would be fighting with Kim over someone she was dating. Learning this information, I had no judgment about his situation. This was not public knowledge at the time. Though Biggie may have been abusive to Lil' Kim, he was kind to me. When no one was giving anyone from Astoria props, Biggie had attended my listening party to promote "Where I Wanna Be Boy." There was a screen airing the video, and T-shirts, and huge Miss Jones posters were hung everywhere. The thrill was when Biggie and Nas got onstage and free-styled. It was a moment in hip-hop history that should have been documented.

"**Look, you** need to let HOT 97 go," my label reps warned, "'cause by you working for them, you're jeopardizing your relationships with radio stations from other clusters. A Radio One or a Clear Channel could resent your attachment to HOT 97 and refuse to let you promote the album. And we can't promote your album effectively, because your program director isn't supporting it."

When I read the spin count at the end of the week, I was devastated. And to make matters worse, when I called Tracy, she didn't come to the telephone, but her assistant, Denine, did, and gave the straight-up truth: "Tracy dropped the record."

"But she just told me she wasn't gonna drop it!"

"Tracy lied to your face," Denine replied matter-of-factly. When I finally reached Tracy, I had words for her, because she tried to play me.

"We are not droppin' the record," Tracy said unconvincingly.

"Denine already told me what's up!" I was furious as I listened to her repeat her lies.

Andre Harrell was out at Motown and word circulated that Kedar Massenburg would replace him. Kedar heavily promoted his artist Erykah Badu and had coined the term "neo-soul." Observing this turn of events, I refused to record. I wrongly assumed that Kedar wanted to clean house and replace the existing talent roster with his own. Neither Doug nor my lawyer counseled me otherwise. Motown never dropped me from their roster, but I felt so isolated from everyone, I wasn't proactive in taking responsibility for what I perceived to be happening.

"**W**hat is such the emergency, Tarsha, that you're tracking me all around Harlem? I told you I had to watch my son!" I was stunned by Doug's tone as I stood on the doorstep of his brownstone.

He had never spoken to me so coldly.

But still, I gathered my words and continued. "I think I'm pregnant."

"Well, if you think you're pregnant, then why don't you go and get a pregnancy test from the drugstore."

Doug had ignored me the whole day. He thought I was calling to try to piss off his child's mother, but I was only trying to call him to let him know about my possible pregnancy.

Why is he being so protective of her? Why is he being so dismissive of me?

As I got back in my car, I thought, *If this is any indication on how this nigga is gonna act, then I'm not tying myself to be with him for the rest of my life.* I called my friend Charisse, canceled our trip to Puerto Rico, and planned my abortion. For four weeks I laid in bed, writhing in pain. I never anticipated the severe depression and abdominal pain that I experienced. My physician prescribed antibiotics and complete bed rest, and except for weekly check-ups, the world did not exist for me. When Doug didn't come by to see me or even try to find out if I was pregnant, memories of his apathy of my hospitalization after my first tour with him occupied my waking hours. And since he didn't ask, I didn't tell him. Even though I was still signed to Motown, I would have to put my career on hold until I healed.

The late rapper Big Pun and I had become close confidants and saw each other nearly every day. Pun hated Doug and thought he was beneath me. "He ain't nothin' but an old-school washed-up rapper! Fuck him! How dare he break your heart!"

Big Pun even cut Doug out of the fuckin' money equation when he told Motown to book me on his tour, plus he did a remix of one of my songs for me and never charged me, forfeiting nearly $50,000.

I began recording again about five weeks later. "2 Way Street" was still the biggest song on *The Other Woman* album. One night, during a twelve-hour conversation, Doug felt comfortable enough to tell me that he was in Jamaica with a bible-toting Christian bitch. He returned with a suitcase of Christian paraphernalia and a new hypocritical perspective on life. Doug liked to shop for religions like people shopped for shoes. In the time we had known each other, he'd sung the praises of the Landmark Forum, a self-help program dedicated to helping people realize their true potential; then when soul legend Isaac Hayes told me about Scientology, I introduced Doug to it; now Doug was back onto Christianity. His hypocrisy was causing my head to spin.

N**o matter** how much I sought Pun's advice, the answer to whatever Doug and I were going through rested with us. My lawyer had stopped returning my telephone calls. And when I would call Doug, he sounded like I was bothering him. When I eventually went to Doug's brownstone, I was stunned that Gigi, one of his babies' mothers, answered the door. I asked to speak to him privately.

"Anything you have to say to me you can say to her," Doug answered, standing in front of Gigi.

"Tell her, Doug. Tell her," Gigi urged in a Nuyorican accent.

"I'm not gonna be with you no more, I'm gonna be with Gigi," Doug said without hesitating.

I didn't argue. I didn't speak. Doug could not have hurt me more if he had cut out my heart and stomped on it. In fact, that may have felt better.

P**iercing tears** didn't kick in until after the shock wore off, and then they refused to stop. As I rocked back and forth on the sofa that Doug had bought, I heard my mother's soothing, yet stern voice: "You are too good for that man. He has got all of those kids. That is not the life for you anyway. He's messy. You don't want a man who is messy, and you don't want a man who got women all over the place and can't commit, so pick up your head and go wash your face. Show them that old Scott blood that you have in you." I never missed my mother more than at that moment. I felt comforted, as if even in death she was protective of me.

Doug broke up with me the day my album was released. June 18, 1998.

And I will never fucking forgive him for that.

It's hard to shake off somebody, like the time spent meant nothing. It meant a lot to me. Still does. Our relationship taught me many invaluable lessons. Among them, never lie down where my security, money, and career might be affected. The more time that separated Doug and me, the more people who I thought were my friends closed their doors.

Timing is a bitch.

When Motown Records no longer made my career a priority, Doug didn't help to create a new record deal. I couldn't get anything from him, on any level. My attorney continued to avoid me, which is why I hate him to this day. The two of them, I really feel, did an injustice to me. The reality was that Doug was, as Big Pun used to say, "the has-been" who benefited from my new celebrity.

This really hurt because though we were not together romantically, I had hoped that Doug and I could continue a business relationship. After too many unreturned telephone calls, I packed up and left the West End Towers apartment, which kept too many memories alive. The lease was in Doug's name and by the time the moving crew had loaded the last box, two months of unpaid rent purposely remained to fuck up his credit.

I was in limbo. My luck had run out. My cash flow dried up. Collection agencies were calling. And I didn't know what I was going to do.

When you feel you have nothing, sometimes you reach for straws. I considered sleeping with Steve Stoute, former president of Urban Music and vice president of Interscope Records, who had been coming after me for a while, and becoming one of those kept women—just to have someplace to stay. I thought about sleeping with Nas and other rappers who had expressed interest, as a means to have money in my pocket. Big Pun threw me a safety net by giving me the first-month deposit on my new apartment. And a new life, without Doug, awaited.

NINE

MY DAILY BREAD

Jonesy's Juice:

Tyra Banks: Tyra always came to an interview prepared and was never thrown by my remarks. She didn't become emotional when I told her that she should never sing on national television. I also respect her transition from being a model to hosting and executive producing two successful television shows. It's obvious that she works hard, diligently researching her topics and doesn't take her opportunity for granted. That being said, neither of her television shows speaks to me. Tyra gives her perspective on issues that she hasn't lived. And she just scratches the surface. Furthermore, her mother's constant presence and seeming expertise on everything is annoying. Tyra needs to come out of Hollywood Hills and get some guests who have lived her show topics. Still, her hustle commands respect.

When I wasn't at HOT 97, I was in the recording studio working on tracks for a future album. Before my 1998 single "Dance Wit Me" was even mixed and mastered, I played it for my program director, Tracy Cloherty. "Um, sounds more like a Mariah type of song than yours," she responded nonchalantly, referencing another relatively new artist on the scene, Mariah Carey. I had reported her feedback to Motown Records, and as a result, the single "2 Way Street" was released first. Tracy's reaction: "It's a great song! We're gonna get it into rotation as soon as a spot opens. I heard it in the hallway, and it sounds good on radio." But when the record label had come to place ads, Tracy played me like she didn't really know me. Like I was some new artist and not one of their own.

HOT 97 had a history of promoting the music of their jocks, but Tracy never supported my music in the way she would support DJs Funkmaster Flex or Angie Martinez. Despite the enthusiasm she had shared with me earlier, the record rotation never exceeded ten spins a week. Tracy played my song "2 Way Street" all of twenty times during the entire summer of 1998.

Before Steve Smith hired me, Tracy was one of the radio programmers who actively sought me out to perform at radio events. But as soon as Tracy saw that Motown Records wasn't behind me, she started disrespecting me. One day, I asked if the HOT 97 van was distributing my promotional material on weekends. Motown had sent a huge box of Miss Jones posters, stickers, single CDs, and postcards to HOT 97. "Yes! Yes!" Tracy said, in a way that implied the stupidity of the question. Then about six months later, a friend in the promotions department called. "You need to come and pick up these CDs, posters, and stuff, because they're about to dump them in the trash."

Other than keeping a hardworking, good weekend jock around or not hurting my feelings, there was no other rationale for Tracy to consistently lie to my face. *It's better to have Miss Jones around, because she's a good fill-in,* Tracy probably thought. And every time Angie Martinez or Wendy Williams was sick, or those two bitches got suspended for scrappin', I was the best fill-in there was. Although Tracy knew that I was a great talent, my music career wasn't on the come-up. She probably felt that doing weekends at HOT 97 was the best thing I ever did.

Honestly, HOT 97 *was* the best thing that ever happened to me.

When **Ed** Lover quit in 1998, Tracy teamed me with DJs Curt Flirt and Steph Lova for the morning show. Tracy said, "The show doesn't sound balanced, 'cause Steph sounds too butch. She holds her own when it comes to conversations about sports with men, but Steph doesn't have that strength when it comes to acting feminine."

Eventually, Steph was fired for almost coming to blows with me in the studio. Then Tracy added the hype man Fat Man Scoop to the show. We would dread when 10:00 A.M. came and our show was over, because that meant a daily verbal morning showdown. Our stomachs would twist and turn 'cause we hated listening with Tracy to a tape of the show.

"Okay, pause it right there. What was that break about? Why do you sound like this? That was not funny. Why would you say that? Start the tape again. Okay, pause. You can't say stupid things like that . . . Don't brand yourselves as the 'New Morning Show,' because I'm still not married to that idea yet," Tracy scolded in one morning-show meeting.

Earlier **that** year, a knuckle-dragging motherfucka began hanging out at HOT 97, wearing tight, high-water pants that emphasized how small his nuts were. His pants barely reached the top of his black, run-over Chuck Taylor sneakers. His name was Troi Torain and he went by the moniker of Star. He began gunning for his own show on the low, but Tracy initially shut him down. She had never heard of him and dismissed anyone who was not a celebrity in her eyes. So Star sold himself as a writer of radio copy, and tried to get on-air by sabotaging Ed Lover's Morning Show with corny, unfunny jokes. When Ed Lover quit, Star wrote for me, Curt Flirt, and Fat Man Scoop, submitting shitty, crappy stuff—worse than what he had turned in to Ed Lover and Dr. Dre. Tracy never took our complaints about Star's work seriously.

"Look, something in there has got to be funny," she would say, in response to our frustration. Tracy and Star were kindred spirits. They shared the same kind of perverse humor. Very sexually depraved and misogynistic. Tracy was into that. She liked that Howard Stern–type shit and listened to Stern every morning.

The criticism from Tracy about our show rolled in like a motorcycle gang on their way to their own Freaknik. Scoop would take the verbal beat-downs, but I would challenge Tracy. She knew that I was serious about my work and that I was only going to take her put-downs for so long. We wanted her to develop our individual talents so we could perfect our on-air characters, but Tracy just bitched and never gave us the tools to be better.

Morning jocks typically work until 12:00 noon, but Scoop and I would often work twelve-hour days, preparing bits and material for the show—without being paid for it. I worked harder then than any other time in my life, even for my albums. Show preparation takes a lot of time. For one bit, my co-host DJ Skeletor and I would write soap operas and then find salespeople to do the voices. We also created interactive games for the listeners. Scoop and Bentley would search their crates to find the perfect record that would work for whatever bit we were creating. We would record, cut it up, loop it, and then get Tracy's approval. Her reaction would be based on how she felt at the moment. 'Cause even if she agreed with something, she might later say, "I didn't like it on the air; don't do it anymore."

We put in the extra hours because we wanted to earn Tracy's approval by showing her that if she believed in us and pushed us, she could have a great team that was just as talented and bright as the *Ed Lover and Dr. Dre Morning Show*. But we needed the criticism to stop and be replaced with professional direction and for her to stop discarding every single idea that we came up with. But Tracy had other ideas. She allowed us to put in unheard-of hours and efforts even though she knew that she already had Star and Buc Wild lined up to replace us. We knew not to call in sick and sacrificed vacations for fear we would lose our jobs. And she knew all along that we weren't what she wanted. But like other radio programmers, Tracy was afraid that if we got wind that she was planning another show, we would step on her to pursue other opportunities before she was able to groom a new team.

Tracy wanted more control than Janet Jackson, and maybe it was because she'd never had anything. She was a perfect example of someone who forgot where they came from. Tracy had been an intern, and then became Steve Smith's music director. When Steve resigned, Tracy assumed the program director position. And she inherited a lot of his staff. This gave her an excuse to clean house of the on-air people, like my friend and fellow broadcaster DJ Red Alert, whom she never wanted in the first place. Tracy became power hungry. Instead of remembering her own struggle to move up, she circled the fucking wagons to become HOT 97's Head Bitch in Charge.

During Tracy's reign, when Diddy wasn't as hot as he'd been in previous years, he became resentful of the disloyalty Tracy showed him. Then Tracy became possessive of Jay-Z. When a rival station, Z100, booked him to perform at their Jingle Ball, Tracy flipped her lid. "HOT 97 is the station that made him. And if he does that concert, he will be sorry." Jay-Z performed at Z100's Jingle Ball, and as a result, his records were temporarily banned from the HOT 97 playlist. The ban didn't last long because HOT 97 couldn't remain a successful hip-hop station without Jay-Z being part of their playlist. It was an example of how Tracy's personal beefs affected HOT 97.

Tracy hated if you maintained your relationships with powerful industry executives. For example, if you mentioned your friend Joe Schmo on the air, and she wasn't chummy with him, you could count on Tracy flying her broomstick into the studio. "Why are you talking about Joe Schmo?"

"I just mentioned him."

"Well, why? We charge for that. It's called a commercial."

But if her Joe Schmo would call Tracy and say, "Hey, Tracy, I'm having a party. Could you have somebody mention it?" then she would say to us, "Mention Joe Schmo's party; nothing formal, just mention it."

She didn't want anybody to get bigger than HOT 97, with the exception of Angie Martinez, who had been Tracy and Steve Smith's pet project. They'd wanted to prove to record executives that they could create stars of their own.

Finally, the ball dropped. Weeks of wondering screeched to a halt.

Damn. Wake up! A new morning show.

"**I**'m taking the 'Morning Show' off next week and I want Star and Buc . . . um, I want you to sit in with them," Tracy announced to me when the shift had ended. Scoop and Bentley were still in the studio working on production.

When my lip lifted itself from the carpet, I protested, "Do you know how awkward that's going to make me feel? Working with Scoop and then I gotta go sit in with Star? That's gonna kill team morale!"

"Do you want the gig or not?" Tracy asked, her voice on edge.

Look, I wanted the gig. I needed the gig. There was no bullshitting that. So I did it.

"Star said that you and he had a run-in back in the day with his little magazine. Said that he wrote some things about you and that you probably wouldn't want to work with him. I told him, I'm sure Miss Jones can get past that. And if she was upset then, being that it was years ago, I know Miss Jones isn't angry now."

Tracy-speak: Jonesy won't be an issue.

Being a very practical woman, I quickly did a cost-net analysis. What would be the ultimate cost and would the net result be losing my job? Envisioning myself losing my beautiful co-op and kinda liking three meals a day, I kept my damn mouth shut. My practical nature doesn't intentionally create an exit for a situation I'm not ready to bounce out of.

One thing is certain: Every dog has its day.

In the next few hours, Tracy led Scoop and Bentley to believe that all was well in what was becoming a house of horrors. "Oh, no, I would never make any changes," she told them. "Star and Buc have never done radio before. Why would I put them in mornings?" So I was torn. Do I tell Scoop and Bentley so they can be prepared for the letdown? And if I do, will they go stomping to Tracy? My conscience tortured me as Ice Cube's "It Was a Good Day" blared through the radio on my desk.

Thanks. But no, it's not.

So, jeopardizing my job, I told Scoop and Bentley. And before the words left my mouth, Bentley, who was the show's producer, went blabbing to Tracy.

"Jonesy told us what's up! Ya know, Tracy, your show is fucked up. Everybody in dere is all fucked up in da head."

Tracy yanked me into her office; her tiny nostrils were flaring. "Do you want this job or not? And why the fuck did you tell them what's going on? You need to learn that loyalty is to yourself first. You're gonna have to learn to be quiet about certain things."

According to Tracy's logic, I had to be loyal to those who had gone out of their way to betray me. When Tracy calmed down, she continued discussing Star and Buc Wild. "I gotta put their names out there in front of yours. I gotta promote these guys hard." With my arms folded across my chest, I wasn't just listening to what she was saying, but to her Tracy-speak—the underlying bullshit was what was important.

Tracy-speak: I don't really give a fuck about you. Just do the news. Be the voice of reason. Be the straight guy.

Fear froze me, so I never came back at Tracy as hard as she was coming at me. I imagined not having a position. And needing a job. So I said whatever needed to be said until she backed off. If I went to jump on Bentley for running to Tracy, I don't remember right now. I was just so relieved that I wasn't getting blown out, and so very sad for my friends.

A week later, Star, who was hanging around in the studio, pulled me to the side and whispered, "You know you're gonna be workin' with me from now on, right?"

"No. Nobody told me," I lied with a straight face, with The Roots and Erykah Badu playing in the background.

"Nobody told you? Well, I'm gonna be taking over this whole thing, and you're gonna be working with me. They payin' me a lot of money. Those white folks are paying me. And you make sure you get what you're supposed to get, 'cause I told them, 'Don't be playin' wit my money!' I went in there and gave them a piece of mind and told them what I wanted." Bentley quit before Star started; he refused to work with him. DJ Skeletor accepted a job in Philly. With Scoop and Bentley gone, and later seeking their fortune in Philly radio and syndication radio, respectively, the morning show that we had put so much sweat into died, and was being replaced with two morons.

As I gathered my belongings in my office, I heard nothing. Tears formed behind my lowered eyelids. My coworkers spoke to me, but I heard nothing. The window shades of the world enveloped me, and I saw only darkness.

Death surrounded me.

That night began a dark, two-week drinking binge. Details and moments still escape me. I was in a fog going to my spot, Caroline's Comedy Club, drinking martinis, or consuming whatever was available. My personal rule had been to never drink on "school nights." But during this time, I drank to dull the pain I felt. I drank by myself, with people, meeting people at the club—wherever and whenever. The toilet and the floor of the bathroom became my best friends. I missed work. And I didn't care, as I drank way beyond my limit. And this was happening every night, because I was so overwhelmed, and so depressed. I felt my life was spiraling out of control. I had done all this work, and now I had to start again from scratch. The effect of Tracy's decision had me depressed days and nights.

To make matters worse, my dear friend Christopher Lee Rios, better known as the rapper Big Pun, died of a massive heart attack. Pun possessed the uncanny intuition to appear on my doorstep whenever I needed a friend. He was twenty-nine years old. I felt like I had died too, and that my heart was under attack. Then George Jackson, Motown president, died of a stroke. I felt as though pivotal people in every arena of my life were leaving. When George was appointed president, he single-handedly restored some of the luster to the label's corporate losses. Teaming up with his partner, Doug McHenry, George produced such shows as *Malcolm and Eddie,* the movie hits *New Jack City* (1991), Kid 'N Play's *House Party 2* (1991) and *House Party 3* (1994), *Jason's Lyric* (1994) and the Martin Lawrence comedy *A Thin Line Between Love and Hate* (1996). Previous to George's arrival, Motown's attention to my career had waned. However, with his arrival, I felt that my music had a new beginning in the hands of this gifted visionary.

During our many conversations, I told Scoop, "I'll never like them . . . don't worry, I'm never gonna be there for Star."

One night, I was so drunk I vomited in Scoop's friend's car, as he drove me home. Scoop followed behind in my silver Mitsubishi Eclipse convertible, the one Doug E. Fresh had given me. I had never been so drunk that I couldn't drive. My friends and family tried to get me to put the brakes on the downward direction my life was taking.

Bentley scolded, "You'd better pull your shit together 'cause you're 'bout to give Tracy a reason to let you go." My binge drinking was a wack attempt to dull my pain, and it was a backward attempt to move forward. Instead of creating positive situations in my life, my drinking only made me want to hide from my fears. It made me struggle out of bed each morning feeling like shit and looking twice my age. The fear of losing everything that I had built—love, great friends and family, music, and a career in radio—snapped me out of binge drinking. I determined to face my challenges rather than seeking consolation in the bottom of a bottle of alcohol, and not to mirror the drinking history of my parents.

The situation at HOT 97 at that moment may not have been all that I wanted it to be, but it damn sure was better than nothing.

I never drank like that again.

"**W**e are not going to do this deal with you. We're going to get somebody else to do the show with Star and Buc, because your lawyer is being difficult. We're tired of going back and forth with him. It's just not worth it," Judy Ellis, the general manager, and Tracy had called to say.

I was vacationing in the Bahamas at the time with my girl Charisse to chill before the show with Star and Buc Wild and I started.

My attorney at the time had reviewed my contract and returned it to Tracy with his comments. "He has all of these red marks. We're not doing this, so you need to work that out." Tracy and Judy didn't want any changes to their contract. What the issues were—termination clause, billing or non-compete provisions—I don't remember.

I phoned New York after my lawyer had left urgent messages to call back immediately. But I felt that since I was on vacation and he was my lawyer, he should just handle whatever needed to be dealt with. My lawyer told me, "Tracy and Judy don't want to negotiate anymore. They took back their offer."

I was on the edge of my bed and Charisse was almost jumping out of hers. "Call dem now! Fuck that! You need your job!" So I called them. Tracy and Judy placed me on speakerphone.

"My lawyer just told me what happened," I said.

"Yeah," one of them said, faking her way to sound sincere. "It was just too much."

"Well, what was he asking for?"

"Look, this is the whole deal: We are willing to give you $65,000 a year." All I had asked for was $75,000, even though Steph Lova was getting $90,000. And then Tracy said, "We're about to start an open search, starting with Coka Lani from Philly. And she's gonna do it."

A loud silence hung in the air between New York and my hotel

room in the Bahamas. Charice was trying to guess which way the conversation was going.

Tracy spoke. "Why are you quiet? Do you want the job or not?"

"Yeah, I want the job!"

"Okay. And we're not going to hear any more from Londell?"

"Yeah. And it's $75,000, right?"

"No, it's $70,000," Tracy blurted out before Judy could answer.
Everyone took a breath.

"We wanted you anyway, Jonesy. Your lawyer was just making it
difficult," one of them said, returning to a sincere bullshit tone.

Their attitudes blew a chill into my vacation. Fo' real.

Star ranted, "I can't stand that lily-livered Fat Man Scoop.
I been asking niggas around here for years to introduce
me to the boss, and nobody wanted to, 'cause they knew once she met
me, what was going to happen—this right here. But you can't stop
greatness! Star and Buc Wild are here, and we got here not by stabbing
our competitors in the back; we ram and stab them right in the front of
their throats. And I'll say this 'bout that Fat Man Scoop, that nigga
never did a damn thing for me . . . all the times I asked him to introduce me to Tracy."

Miguel, the board operator, who had done nothing spectacular with
his life but drive the HOT 97 van, and Buc, Star's brother, laughed
nervously, exposing their cavities like they were in the front row at *Def
Comedy Jam.*

And wasn't shit funny.

This was Day One.

The truth: Scoop had personally walked Star into Tracy's office and
made the introduction. But Star got more mileage by saying that shit on
the air whether it was true or not. And Tracy didn't care enough about
office morale to stop Star's ranting. At Emmis Broadcasting, the cardinal rule we had all been made to live by was to never talk about our co-

workers on-air. Well, Star came in and shot that shit right out the window. His ranting about Scoop made me very uncomfortable, and I didn't know at the time that Scoop had hooked Star up with Tracy. When I found out, I thought Star was crazy for not admitting that.

Saying you stabbed Scoop in the front of his neck, after you took the man's job. Trifling!

Buc Wild began to not appreciate being the butt of Star's lame-ass attempt to tell jokes. Buc and I would shoot dice when we weren't on the air, while Star complained about management and scribbled on his writing pad. When Buc lost, he paid up, and when I lost, I paid up. When Star would get involved in the dice game, he'd raise the bets astronomically. One time he lost $5K to $7K to me, and didn't pay his debt.

One afternoon, broadcaster Funkmaster Flex interviewed the singer Ginuwine, who kept asking who I was and for a quick introduction. To which I paid no mind. Ginuwine was a talented singer, a handsome guy, but I really wasn't checking for him. Flex said, "Jonesy, ain't nothin' wrong with showing up at his promotion party and gettin' some press shots with him." Before I could get introduced to him, Ginuwine blurted on the air, "I want Miss Jones to come to my party and wear my favorite color, red." I smiled when I heard about it, and said, "Fuck it! I'm going."

That night I wore the sexiest red dress that I had, with red pumps, and made my grand entrance at the Deep nightclub. Ginuwine's mouth dropped to the floor when he saw me. He gave me a warm welcoming hug and requested that we take photos together. Telephone numbers were exchanged and we spoke a few times, but I never expected anything in terms of a relationship.

Solé began as a glorified groupie and became a publicity whore who wanted Ginuwine as if her very life depended on it. At this time, he was not involved with her, she was trying to coerce him to be. She threw herself at him. Everywhere he performed, she would try to get booked at the same venue. To the point that everywhere he went, there she was.

All females were considered a threat, and what facts Solé didn't possess she manufactured in her paranoid mind. I never pursued Ginuwine. He pursued me. But we were never a couple; we enjoyed being artists who were friends. I wasn't trying to make a connection with him. He was just a friend. It was never a passionate energy. There needs to be communication on other levels. I learned that from my affair with Busta Rhymes.

And if it were more than friendship, I would be woman enough to say so.

When HOT 97 held a promotional event in Montego Bay, Jamaica, Ginuwine was slated to perform and asked me to meet him at the resort. He was excited about being nominated for the upcoming American Music Awards. We worked together as he practiced his acceptance speech. Later, when Solé appeared on broadcaster Angie Martinez's show, instead of promoting her music, Solé used valuable media time to talk shit about me. When I was told what was happening, I called in live to the show. Solé's position was that she just wanted to be heard, but Angie's show wasn't a therapist's couch.

"First of all, we don't need to be arguing, because he ain't with you," I said.

"No, no . . . he is with me, he is with me!" Solé emphasized, like anyone truly cared.

"Sweetheart, I have a hot bubble bath with my name written on it," I responded, caring less about Ginuwine and Solé than paint drying.

That on-air episode went down in history as a "Solé told Miss Jones off" moment. But when you think about it, did she really? Because it was clear to those who knew that Ginuwine had pursued a friendship with me. An item appeared in Jamie Foster Brown's rag tabloid *Sister*

2 *Sister* magazine. Jamie never reports from both sides of the story. She could have easily called to verify if the rumor was legit.

Now that Ginuwine and Solé are married, I hope she's grateful that he helps her take care of the three kids that she had with Sam "It's on Tonight" Salter, an R&B artist who knocked her up back in the day. Ginuwine has never disrespected or played me out. He has said, "No disrespect to you, Jonesy, but every time Solé hears your name she gets an attitude and it causes a problem. So please don't think that it's me trying to be disrespectful. I just don't feel like hearing her mouth!"

"Ooh, Tarsha, I like him for you," Charisse said, pointing at the guy onstage at Caroline's Comedy Club. It was the HOT 97 Gong Show night, and I was the host. The magician had pulled this cute brother out of the audience to participate in a magic trick. He was really funny when he interacted with the magician onstage.

With Charisse egging me on, and me kinda liking him, I went over to him after the show. His name was Bernard, a tall, striking-looking brother.

Charisse began with the interrogation. Bernard seemed to take her meddling in stride. And of course I was as interested in his answers as she.

"Where do you live?

"Are you married?

"What do you do?" Bernard said he was a filmmaker.

"Are you interested in a career in music, in any capacity?"

"No, not at all," Bernard answered, as if that was the furthest idea from his mind. It was a deal-breaker for me, to date men who were trying to break into the business. Breakin' on my ass was not what I was looking for. I wanted a man in my life who would love me as his woman, not as a gatekeeper to Bad Boy Records or some shit. And wondering and questioning is something I don't like to do.

"How many kids do you have?"

When Bernard said that he had more than one child, me and Charisse were like, "Thanks, but no thanks!" But Bernard jumped back in with, "Hey! But I got my situation under control!" Charisse and I chuckled in response, just as one of the managers of Caroline's asked to see me to confirm the comedic lineup. When I returned, Charisse had returned to our table and was chatting with some people seated behind her. In the meantime, a chick that I immediately recognized as Carla, whose ass I had to twice beat from Music & Art, was chatting up Bernard. Rumor had it that after high school, she'd developed an illustrious career as the neighborhood jump-off that everyone could just go and fuck. When Bernard saw me, he shut her down and returned his attention to me. As Bernard and I sat with Charisse, she whispered, "That girl been eyeballing us all night, trying to get your attention . . . I thought you saw her." I felt both triumph and pity for Carla. If she had not participated in my beat-downs in high school, she could have easily shared in my success.

Charisse leaned back in her chair and applauded the comedian taking the stage. In the meantime, Bernard scribbled his telephone number, and I followed suit. He was excited when I finally called the following Friday. We chatted for a while, and I then invited him back to Caroline's Comedy Club, where he met my friend Rhonda.

After dealing that morning with Star's bullshit, I looked forward to being with a man who was funny and down to earth. Bernard met me in front of Caroline's, rested his arm on the back of my chair, but for the most part was quiet the rest of the evening. Rhonda nodded her approval; her judgment was just as off as mine.

If Bernard had joined in the chatter at the table, we would have known right then that he was simple. And simple is as simple does, because as complicated and volatile as my life was at that time, that was exactly what I needed. Bernard liked staying in the house all day. He wasn't one of those guys who would all of a sudden say, "I'll be back," and spend the bulk of the day in the street, while you're paging his stupid ass. I had gotten out of a relationship with Doug E. Fresh with that shit.

After the show, where all our food and drinks were on the house because of my relationship with Caroline's, Bernard walked me to my car, and we shared a kiss. All of that was cool, however, what bothered me right away—but which I proceeded to ignore—was that Bernard didn't pay for my parking. That really fucking annoyed me. I ignored the beginning of his pattern of cheapness. I didn't listen to my stomach back then—my intuition. And I'm just now beginning to listen to it and stop second-guessing myself.

We spent hours in our mutual beds talking about our lives, our pasts, and how he wound up retired from the Corrections Department. Bernard explained how he impregnated a sixteen-year-old girl while he was with his child's mother. (Yet another sign I chose to ignore.) We watched television, listened to music and took drives around Manhattan. Bernard was a former sex addict and introduced me to Bishop TD Jakes, as he had become very spiritual. Together we would watch the entire TD Jakes video library while we ate popcorn in bed.

When we first had sex, three weeks later, it took place without planning or a shred of romance. It was horrible, because it was not lovemaking, and Bernard cried afterward. Flashbacks of my parents' living room and Calvin fumbling with his ten seconds of manhood occurred. Frankly, I had expected more. Bernard had set me up to expect more. In my mind, this chocolate brother, with the deep voice that he knew how to flex, was going to put it on a sister. I had imagined that I would have difficulty walking after one of our forays. To make it worse, I had to act like Dr. Phil to massage his damaged ego, while I pretended that my sexual drive had been satisfied. "You don't know what it's like to get the woman of your dreams—that you been dreaming about all of these years—and you can't perform. You don't know," he cried, sitting on the edge of my king-sized bed.

We didn't date in the traditional sense. Any of our nights on the town were on the dime of either HOT 97 or crazy-ass me. Bernard never planned anything. Every restaurant was in my world and we were in venues from my life. Bernard wasn't worldly—which made sense, since he lived in his mother's basement in Queens. There were no conversations about global events, things read in a book or newspaper, issues that mattered beyond our world. "Dat nigga Star is crazy. I heard him this morning," Bernard would say, as he thumbed the PlayStation nearly all day long. Searching for a diversion from my random thoughts about Doug, Bernard liked being silly and he didn't drink or smoke weed.

Bernard would gas up my car and take out the trash. He would do things that a man does for his woman. And I had never had that before. I appreciated it. It was masculine. And because Bernard was a homebody, and my work at the radio station kept me in the world, I welcomed the quiet refuge with him from the craziness I experienced on a daily basis. I needed a safe, regular brother without the drama.

Even though my deal with Motown was over, I hadn't given up on my music career. I secured a writer's publishing deal with Derrick Thompson, vice president of Urban Music, BMG Songs, and was in the studio cranking out lyrics nearly 24/7. Bernard complained that we weren't getting enough time to spend together, and I adjusted my schedule so that we could spend the evenings chillin'. About a month later, as I came out of the bathroom, Bernard had set up my radio to play a cassette of a group he managed. *A group he managed* echoed in my head. Upset and confused, I told Scoop and Bentley, while Star was in another studio telling someone how great he was. It was unanimous. They were like, "Get rid of him now."

But that was not what I wanted to hear. I would've preferred them kicking some shit like, "It's no big deal. Stop trippin' and go be wit da brotha. There ain't nothin' for you to worry about." But Scoop and Bentley kept repeating themselves, "Get rid of him now." I thought that they were overreacting. So I stayed with Bernard, thinking that

Scoop and Bentley didn't know what the hell they were talking about. And kept both of them out of the loop of my personal business.

"Don't hold it against me—the fact that I've been managing this group. I'm not even hands-on with it. My partner handles everything." And I continued to ignore the rumblings in my stomach.

TEN

STAR OF THE LION'S DEN

Jonesy's Juice:

Jay-Z: One evening, Jay-Z, Def Jam Promotions VP Mike Kaiser and I were behind the velvet ropes at some HOT 97 event. Mike and I kept the banter going because Jay-Z didn't seem to know how to string words together when he wasn't rapping. He was talented but had no flavor. Then out of nowhere, Jay turns and stares at my ass and says, "Big girls can't take it like little girls can."

"What? How do you know that? Is it a theory you're working from?" I asked.

"Trust me, I know," he snickered. After that revelation, Jay-Z returned to being dull. Since then, he may have gained fortune and made some great business moves, but in the personality department, he's still lacking and makes for a very boring interview.

Tracy glanced into the studio. Our interview with Jay-Z stank like a Staten Island landfill. Star was trying to prove to the world that not only was he a hater, but he could hate on the most popular rapper there was.

Jay-Z came into the station not having met Star before. He knew me. But I had to fall back because it was Star's interview. And Star, since he was anti-Jay-Z, asked insulting questions that didn't relate to Jay-Z, his music, or his life. So Jay-Z totally disconnected from Star and ignored the insulting questions.

Dead silence.

Jay-Z didn't play into Star's game by responding.

A second of silence on radio feels like an eternity. It sounds like something is wrong.

"Take control of the interview. Take control," Tracy whispered in my ear.

Star was like, "I'm not changing who I am." Star didn't try to bail out of the sinking ship—he simply continued with his awkward line of questioning.

Jay-Z promised Tracy, "I will never do this show again." And his word has been his bond. Jay-Z has not granted interviews for my show either.

Star continued antagonizing Scoop on the air, and then he dissed Funkmaster Flex. He acted like an obsessed punk and sweated them every morning like Cain sweated Abel, even though they worked other parts of the day. Star would come in the studio in the morning and search the trash can. Then, on the air, he would pull records out the trash can and turn to Miguel, his lackey. "Miguel, who was in the studio last night?"

"Um, 10:00 to 12:00 A.M.? That was Flex."

"Oh, so Flex is throwing a Mobb Deep record in the trash can?"

Tracy put a stop to that in a morning-show meeting. "Stop talking about Flex. Stop it." Tracy and Flex had a different relationship. She let Flex do his thing because he was her power; he ran the station. Flex's show earned a ten percent market share—that's at least two million listeners each day. Flex also brought enormous street cred, being the first DJ to distribute hip-hop mix tapes; he had the ability to make or break an up-and-coming artist. Tracy took credit for

Flex's status and rode the wave of his success. Whatever Flex wanted to do in terms of promotions or adding new music to playlists got done.

Star tried to lie and play it off. "You tell Flex to stop talking about me."

"Flex doesn't talk about you. But I'll tell him not to, if he has."

I was hired to be the voice of reason. But you could tell Star wanted me to be a Robin Quivers to his version of Howard Stern. I'd never listened to Howard Stern, so I didn't know who Robin was. I had no idea that there was somebody that he was patterning himself after, until Star began making references to Howard Stern during the show. And even behind the mike, Star would drone on about how he always wanted to be the black Howard Stern. He wanted a female who agreed with him more often than not. He liked when I laughed with him. But then Tracy would check me to get back into character. If I believed, for example, what he said about Mary J. Blige being "a drop out, alcoholic bitch, rocked over and this and that," there were times when I would join with him and start mocking Mary's singing. Star would just fall out laughing. Tracy told me my role was not to agree with Star. "The show isn't sounding balanced, Jonesy. I know you're a bigger hater than Star, so remember your role."

But when I did what Tracy wanted, Star would shut me down. "Turn her mic off." In response I would speak loudly in the background. When I stepped to him about it in front of Tracy, he would pretend that he was joking. In private, Tracy would say, "Jonesy, you need to get a thicker skin. This is just his shtick. He doesn't really mean it. Look, I know it's hard. No one wants to work with him. You're the only one who's willing."

Star continued his antics. The tension continued to build. And he became more clever.

Star began characterizing me on the air in ways that turned some of the audience against me. Referring to me as the "High Maintenance Miss Jones . . . she doesn't accept less than," he created an image of me that the public wanted to hate. Star pretended that he was "biggin' me up," when he was really just *setting me up*.

He began taking messages off the voice mail and editing them to make it sound like the audience hated me. Star periodically aired negative "Miss Jones" voice-mail messages. Coincidentally, this would occur when I was holding my own, getting comfortable or had gotten a laugh.

Star was a very smart man. He dated only young girls. Men do that because they need to control somebody, and it's usually young girls who are vulnerable to that kind of manipulation. When Star first started at the station, he was dating a young woman whose parents *allowed* him to date her. He got her braces, straightened out her credit, treated her like she was a "project," a fixer-upper. He was building her into the image he wanted. Because of the pimp in him, he knew how to break a bitch down.

I had never before met somebody as offensive as Star. Scoop and I would play with each other, saying occasionally insulting stuff, and if we didn't agree, it didn't create any beef. But Star was constantly setting me up to fall.

One morning the streets were talking about Bobby—the marijuana that was found in Whitney's purse at an airport in Hawaii. I went on a rant about how Bobby was bringing out the worst in her. I also read from a tabloid that she kept her drugs in a black onyx box. When I arrived home my telephone was ringing off of the hook—Lionel Ridenhour, who was then executive vice president at Arista Records, had Whitney on a conference call.

"I thought we were friends," Whitney yelled, obviously stoned, as I had never met her in my entire life. "How dare you talk about me! You don't know me! Where is your utopia? Bobby is Bobby and men are going to do things. I love him and he loves me and we are going strong." I didn't respond. I was just shocked that Whitney Houston was on my telephone. I calmly listened and then invited Whitney to come on the show.

"I would love to. I'll bring Bobby and Bobbi Kristina," Whitney responded.

When I told Star, he downplayed booking Whitney, drowned my excitement, and disrespected her so hard on the air that she refused to be interviewed.

In his head, the show was totally his house. His retaliation was like a sucker punch, and whittled away at my self-esteem. You never knew when it was coming, but when it did, it was like inhaling ammonia. I assumed the stance of a boxer, never knowing when and where it was going to come from.

The work environment became increasingly hostile. I finally stood up at a morning-show meeting and said, "I'm not takin' this shit no more." And Buc Wild, Miguel, and Sergeant Reggie, who contributed sports, began telling me that Star was plotting behind my back.

"Yo, Jonesy, Star is monitoring you."

"Yo, Jonesy, Star goes and tells Tracy that you're comin' in late."

"Yo, Jonesy, Star told Tracy that you were on your two-way pager during the show."

"Watch your back, Jonesy. Um tellin' you, this cat is tryin' to set you up," Miguel would say.

"Watch your back. Watch your back, Jonesy," Sergeant Reggie warned. I had recommended Reggie to do sports, and he was returning the favor.

Their warnings stayed with me.

Rapper Queen Pen and I became close friends. She and I were and continue to be kindred spirits. As a teen, Queen Pen grew up in a Brooklyn housing project and was discovered by producer Teddy Riley. She and I started to hang out after the release of her 1997 debut album, *My Melody*. Queen Pen is an old-school chick, loyal to the core, and believes in handling any deserving retribution on her own terms. Generous with her time and knowledge, Queen would often mentor newcomers to the industry, especially newbie women.

When rapper Foxy Brown was trying to break into the music industry, Queen Pen took her under her wing, helping her with her rhymes, offering advice during extended telephone conversations, everything from stage presence to introductions to powerful music executives and, in fact, Foxy lived with Queen Pen for a short time.

As Foxy became more popular, her true nasty personality began to emerge. She started believing her own hype and misdirected her nastiness to those who had helped her gain any success. Foxy began boasting, "I'm the nicest rapper out of all female rappers. I mean, *all* of them—all of the queens, all of them."

Foxy and I were as cool as anyone could be with her. You never know if she values you for you or because of your standing in the music industry. But Queen Pen was heated and felt that Foxy was disrespecting her music all over the town. Queen felt Foxy had used her. Now that she was gaining a little notoriety she was giving Queen her ass to kiss. Their feud soon spilled out and became the buzz of the streets. During a talent showcase at Medgar Evers College, Foxy and I sat together during the proceedings. Queen Pen saw me and tried to enter the row of seats. But once she saw bigmouthed Foxy, Queen scrambled to jump in her face, to the point of everyone trying to restrain her. Foxy didn't want any part of a confrontation with Queen and exited the row of seats in the opposite direction. Even though Foxy escaped that time, she kept bad-mouthing the enraged Queen Pen. At a Reno music convention, Queen kicked Foxy so hard that she fell, and had to use crutches. Queen had tried to squash the noise between them, however, and had even reached out to Foxy, who seemingly wanted to keep shit going.

Once Queen saw Foxy parked on a Brooklyn street and again attempted to bring a truce. "Can I talk to you for a minute?" Queen asked.

"No, you can't talk to me about nothing!" Foxy answered sarcastically. Queen Pen lunged into Foxy's window and snatched her out of the car, beating her down in the middle of the street.

Finally, after years of no contact, in August 2004 Foxy Brown extended an olive branch to Queen Pen, at Russell Simmons's Annual Hip-Hop Summit in Detroit, Michigan. "I want to extend an olive branch [to someone with] whom I have had a rivalry," Foxy said to a packed auditorium. The two women then hugged to a roomful of applause.

"**W**hat's up with these twenty-minute conversations with your baby's mother?" Bernard and I were on a double date with Charisse and her boyfriend, Danny, then Bernard got an emergency telephone call. He had to rush to his baby mother's house and check on his daughter. But of course, he explained, "I take care of my daughter but I'm not wit her motha. I'm wit you."

The clock on my nightstand ticked away—one, two, then three hours. Bernard didn't return that night. And I was devastated. It took every ounce of strength to drag myself out of bed the next morning to go to work. Usually, the night before I download some late-breaking prep for the show, but this time I hadn't been able to move. The apartment was dark except for the one light in the living room near the front door. I rationalized that I hadn't invested much in the relationship with Bernard. "Chalk it up to experience, or something positive," I tried to encourage myself.

"Please, I'm sorry. Shit happens. Please, I have kids," Bernard begged when he returned the next day. And with his sweet promises, my anger evaporated. Our honeymoon periods were always fresh and romantic, temporarily quieting the rumblings in my stomach.

The euphoria continued when Bernard kneeled in a limo and proposed to me in front of his friends as we returned home from an event I'd hosted. Hesitantly, I accepted, with a less than enthusiastic "I guess so." Bernard, though usually a non-drinker, had been drinking, so I thought he was drunk.

"Why would you hesitate? Oh, shit! You gonna play me out in front of my boys? I can't get a yes?" he asked.

"All right. I guess so." I shrugged. I was not the image of a thrilled newly engaged woman.

Our next speed bump came faster. I must have felt it coming.

"I wanna use your name to promote a boat ride," he told me. "I'll do all of the work."

Of course, he didn't. I used my name to hire the comedian, to get a discount on the boat, to print flyers. And the next thing I knew, I was running around town handling his business while he went to the movies.

"I'm here with my daughter."

"Who the fuck do you think you are? You're using me. Here I am doing all the work, and then you're going to want to split the money. Don't you think I want to be in a movie theater? I deserve to be—I'm the one being used."

"You know what? I don't love you anymore," Bernard yelled.

Bernard never gave me a chance to fall in love with him, as more and more of his projects became linked with the use of my name and connection with HOT 97. I cared for him, but there was something in my gut that I just couldn't shake.

Bernard continued to spend more time at my apartment, leaving only to go back to his mother's house in Queens for a change of clothing, until finally he moved in. We discussed what my monthly expenses were, and he agreed to pay half of the rent. And he did—for one month. After that, there were monthly excuses why he couldn't pay.

And every day, I felt more and more resentful. Our arguments became centered on his kids, his baby's mother, his sixteen-year-old baby mother, and his PlayStation. Bernard just wasn't ready for what he put himself into. He behaved as if people and projects outside of our relationship were more important. After a few months, I decided to withhold his share of the profits from the boat rides.

"How you gonna take the money? That's money I was gonna——"

"Well, you're supposed to pay rent. And I got shit to do too," I responded. We didn't speak for a bit. But then Bernard was back to "Can I take your car?" He would let his baby's mother use his car and he'd use mine. And resentment piled on top of frustration, because he kept me a secret from his youngest child's mother. Irony is a bitch—as she listened to the morning show, and heard me talk about the new man in my life, who rubs my feet, gases my car, and has proposed. When the bomb was laid on her that Bernard was the man in my life, her face was cracked.

"Don't you think you need to be going with me so we can show her that we're a couple?" I asked Bernard as he tried to rush out of the door on Christmas morning.

"I don't want that uncomfortable feelin' in my mother's house. You just tryin' to set it off. You just wanna make Latice feel bad."

"So it's okay to wanna make me feel bad by trying not to make her feel bad? You're not gonna do it!"

Instead of my man, Bernard was basically my chauffeur; I paid him $100 for each drive. He would place the money in a jar in the kitchen. "This money is for both of us, when we need it." He obviously felt that was all the contribution he needed to make. One hundred damn dollars.

Speed bump.

Though Bernard was an expert with PlayStation, he didn't know how to disconnect the telephone. During his boat-ride scam, he left a recording on my cell phone, of a conversation he had with his running buddy. He told the guy his version of what happened after he'd stayed out late the night before.

"Hell, no, I didn't get in trouble. Man, I wear the pants in the house. She don't tell me what to do. I run shit. And I told her, if she don't like it, she can get the fuck out."

His buddy laughed. "Yo, you said that? And what did she say?"

"Other than 'I'm glad you came home,' she didn't say nothin'. Man, I'm like 'Get the fuck outta here.' And I went and sat down and watched television."

In reality, this stranger in *my* house, who was in fact paying no rent, was checked the moment he came through my front door.

So I set him up.

It was a beautiful afternoon to go jewelry shopping for my man at the Green Acres Mall in Valley Stream. When we arrived at the jewelry story, he was like a kid at Disneyland. He hovered over the display cases, meticulously choosing a variety of necklaces. I said, "Don't worry about the price. Go ahead and get what you want." With glee all over his face, Bernard finally selected the necklace he wanted.

"Hold on, I gotta make a phone call," I said, as he was modeling in the mirror of the store.

When I accessed the message, I played his conversation with his friend back and held the cell phone up to his ear. Bernard didn't know whether to open or close his mouth. He didn't know whether to walk or run. "Take that shit off of your neck, and act like you know. You're an embarrassment. You do stupid things for no reason," I said, storming out of the jewelry store.

"You're overreacting! You don't even know what that was about!" Bernard said, trotting behind me to make sure I didn't leave his ass stranded at the mall. He didn't know whether to be mad, although he was, or continue looking stupid, which he did.

But the Big Payback was far from over. When we returned to my apartment, I dialed his buddy and told Bernard to pick up the telephone in the living room.

"You walked in the door because . . . ?" I said.

"Because I begged to come back home," a remorseful Bernard said.

"And once your pathetic ass came back home, you did what?"

"I walked in the house. Stayed quiet and kept to myself."

"Why?"

"Because I knew that you didn't feel like being bothered with my bullshit."

"And just for the record, a woman will, and always will, wear the pants in this relationship . . . and do you like it that way?"

"Yes, I like it that way."

Bernard's friend, instead of laughing his ass off, like he'd done during Bernard's version of the story, didn't have a word to say. It was as if I was kicking both their asses.

August 27, 2001.

As with most morning-show teams, we never met in advance to develop show prep. We voiced our obligatory promotions and commercials, but as for creating together as a team, that never happened. Star always planned everything and kept the content of each day's show a clandestine secret. I was specifically responsible for the gossip, and if there was a guest, for preparing the interview questions. I was afloat without support from management, but I knew that victory comes to those who persevere.

On August 25, the telephone lines remained lit all morning as fans of the late singer Aaliyah called to share their grief and condolences over her death in a tragic plane crash in the Bahamas. Some listeners could barely put any words together before they burst into tears. To Star, it was just another day. And he was trying to shed his boredom.

Buc Wild was on vacation. Crossover Reese, the official ass-kisser and radio groupie, piped up: "Star! If you wanna really move the needle and get David Hinckley, the *Daily News* media reporter, talking, and this whole city talking, then this is what you need to do!" Star listened intently to Reese's idea. Reese and Miguel had already put together the sound effects of a woman's bloodcurdling screams. He'd also air the sounds of a loud crash.

"I don't want no part of it," I told everyone; I got jive-ass smirks in response. "I don't think you should do it. And if you do, I'm gonna leave." Mocking Aaliyah's tragedy was not what I represented, then or now.

Ultimately, Star got on the air and said, "Uh, I was about to do somethin' tasteless, but Miss Jones is against it. She doesn't want me to do it. So I'm not gonna do it." Then all of a sudden, sounds of a plane crash and a woman screaming broadcast all over the Tri-State area. I felt like a brick had hit me.

On the air, I said to Star, "I wish that were you on the plane instead of her." I rose and screamed, "I hate you," and then stormed out of the studio.

Aaliyah represented me. She was a solo artist who got on a plane to perform in a video and didn't make it back home. Who's to say that couldn't have been me on that plane? Aaliyah and I were cool. She never created drama for nobody. Aaliyah was always the one who would do something silly, crack a joke, bust a fart or play a practical joke. She was not a phenomenal singer or an artist who would change music. She was not an Alicia Keys. But she was mad cool, and she never bothered anybody. Her connection to R. Kelly got her noticed, but beyond that her appeal was that she sang pure, soft, like an angel. I had interviewed her for Russell Simmons's now defunct 360 Hip Hop website in the Hamptons. She had arrived in a private helicopter with Damon Dash and Jay-Z. I later learned she was dating Damon Dash. When I came on the music scene, Aaliyah was one of the first artists that I met. It wasn't like it is now, where the industry is flooded with a million female solo artists. There were just a few back then—Aaliyah, Brandy, and Mary J.

When she died, Aaliyah was starting in movies. Her flower was just blooming. She would probably be a movie star right now, even on the superstar level. Her last movie, *Queen of the Damned,* was on schedule for theatrical release. Aaliyah was from our genre of music, our generation. She was us.

Crying, I went into Tracy's office to tell her what had happened. She replied with a stern face, "You're wrong. You don't ever wish death on your coworkers. You owe him an apology. Go in there and apologize." Tracy completely ignored what Star had done.

She thought that I was wrong and didn't care about what he'd done. She hadn't heard the show. All she needed was for me to put out a potential fire with Star. That was her MO the entire time Star worked for her. "Keep Star happy. Keep Star happy." Tracy would tell Fat Man, "Scoop, I don't care if Star talks about you on the radio. If you say something back to him, I'm firing you."

It was difficult for me to do something I was against. But because I wanted to keep my job, I said, "Okay." My feet moved like lead. Nikki, who booked guests for KISS-FM, our Emmis sister station, asked if I was okay, and she walked with me back to the studio, trying to make me feel better.

Do other female cohosts go through this shit?

When I reached the studio, I stood at the door, and said to Star, "I'm sorry about what I said." I apologized, but not because I meant it. The apology was just to cover my ass, in case Tracy asked Star about it later.

It wasn't until that afternoon that Tracy and Judy realized the shit had hit the fan. And it was bigger than Tracy had thought it was going to be. It was bigger than Judy had thought it was going to be. Especially when the telephones started ringing with calls from angry listeners. Advertisers pulled their commercials, and dollars flew out the window. Judy and Tracy were shocked that black folks gave a shit when jokes were made about the death of one of their own.

I was drained. Later that afternoon, my phone rang at home. It was Tracy.

"Um, we have a problem. This thing is more serious than we thought. We don't know exactly what to do. Do you have any ideas? How we can spin this? We're taking Star off the air for a little while until things cool down."

My mind spinned as I listened to her. Just a few hours earlier, I was made to feel like I had done something wrong. Now here she was, trying to pick my brain for ideas to save her ass. "Whatever you say, Tracy. Whatever has to be done."

Tracy continued, sounding like the wind had been knocked out of her. "I'd like you to fill in for Star, because people are lovin' you right now. You're the hero. Use that sentiment to get love for Star and soften the blow. Keep reminding people that Star did apologize at the end."

That was Tracy's entire purpose. She never apologized to me, and I felt she had missed the damn point, that she had lost her focus on what was important. She still thought that black folks were overreacting. "White people make jokes about death all the time. There are great stand-up comedians who do it and make it their routine."

Aaliyah ain't no joke. Don't this bitch get it?

Star was suspended on August 28, 2001. As the avalanche of complaint e-mails and faxes continued rolling in, Star phoned me at home to see what was going on.

"Uh, Miss Jones . . . Star. What are they sayin' about me up there? Are they talkin' about lettin' me go? Uh. Uh, what do ya got planned for tomorrow? What's goin' on with you?"

This was not the first time Star had phoned me after-hours. From those conversations, when he was at his most vulnerable, I understood that he always felt he'd never been given a chance at anything. I'd seen that side of him. He tried to sell the other side—the hard, sarcastic side—so hard, but I could only buy so much. That's when I knew that all the shit he talked about being the "hater" and not giving a fuck about anything . . . That's when I knew Troi "Star" Torain really wanted to be loved. And if he was hated, he wanted to be hated on his own terms.

The brother is shook. Shook like Jell-O.

Star returned to the air on September 10, 2001.

ELEVEN

TUMBLING DOWN

A friend called my cell phone during the show. "Jonesy! Did you hear about the plane crashing into the World Trade Center? Is it true?"

Star looked at me, wondering what was going on. It was my understanding that the crash involved a personal plane. Not that a commercial airliner had actually flown through one of the towers. It was September 11th. Once we realized something tragic was definitely happening, we didn't know if we should go on the air with it, because the facts were still sketchy.

Judy and Tracy ran past the studio, toward the program director's office. We were confronted with how serious it was when they joined Star and me in the morning-show office, and we watched as the second plane hit. Star bugged out. Tracy and Judy asked if we minded going back on the air to calm the listeners and relay news updates. Star agreed.

After the first ten minutes back on the air, Star started buggin' again like a crazy man. "I got to get the fuck outta here. I gotta make sure my moms is all right." He just lost his mind and left, with Buc Wild in tow.

Thank God for Lisa Evers, host of HOT 97's "Street Soldiers." She and the rest of the staff pitched in and worked round-the-clock shifts. I was fatigued from monitoring my father's—Billy's—worsening health, so I was relieved when Star bounced, 'cause then it was okay for me to leave. My car was the only one on the West Side Highway, and I was able to get uptown without walking.

I felt so bad for the people of this city and especially those who were injured or who had lost their lives. Arriving home, all of the news came through the television. I saw the cries of people needing help. Help to find their loved ones. Help for food. I asked Bernard to go with me to donate food to people.

"Don't worry about people. Handle your own business."

September 11th made everybody stop thinking about poor Aaliyah. And Tracy and Judy were hearing very few protests about Star being back on the air, as they secretly renegotiated his contract.

Because of how the listeners had reacted to me after the Aaliyah incident, Star felt threatened and had been planting seeds that I was not a team player. Meanwhile, Tracy kept telling me, "Yes, we're gonna renew your contract. And I'm gonna give you $90,000 a year."

Impatiently, I wondered, *When? When?*

Soon after, during a morning-show meeting in Tracy's office, someone suggested creating a Star and Miss Jones feature, and then adding Buc Wild. Star went ballistic. "There will never be a Star and Miss Jones. Get the fuck outta here. It's the 'Star and Buc Wild Morning Show,' " Star shouted.

I lost my cool and left the room. "Enough is fucking enough!"

"Jonesy, come back in here. You don't walk outta meetings like that!" Tracy yelled. I went back into her office.

"I don't care!" Star yelled. "Let her walk! I'm tired of tiptoeing around her feelings. I don't have to work with nobody where I gotta watch what I say. I been nothin' but respectful of Miss Jones ever since I got here. You gotta make a decision. It's gotta be me or Miss Jones." Then *he* stormed out.

"Go talk to him! Go talk to him!" Tracy begged.

"Why do I have to talk to him? You're the boss!"

"It's his show."

"Since when? You said it's all of our show."

"If you guys can't get along, then I'm going to have to make a decision. And I'll have to go with Star, 'cause he brings the ratings."

"Oh, yeah? Well, what do I bring? And how do you decide why people listen and who they're liking more?"

"Go talk to Star," she urged.

Then her boss, Judy, got involved. "Kiss his ass. We women in corporate America have to do that all the time. Making men feel like they're smarter than they actually are. Look, whatever you have to say to him to get back on that show, then you need to do it. Call him. Have a meeting. Say whatever you have to say."

Next they're gonna tell me to suck his dick.

I called Star. "I'm sorry. My walking out was an overreaction. I think we need to sit down and talk."

He listened and then tried to act real hurt and disappointed. "All right, I'll get back to you, Miss Jones."

So I was in limbo. This was a setup. Everything Star wanted, he got.

Star and I met that weekend in front of his house. I pulled up in my truck, and Star got inside. "I've really enjoyed working with you. I love you, Miss Jones. I love you, but the guys . . . they don't think you're down for the team. It's the rest of the show. Not me. So I don't know what to tell ya. You take care of yourself," Star said, and he got out of the truck.

I phoned Tracy. "What does that mean?" she asked.

"You're the boss. You ask him!"

She called him and then called me back. "I don't wanna talk to him too soon. Seems like he's still mad." Tracy was being worked by Star. When he didn't get his way, he would have temper tantrums and turn over furniture during meetings. And he was never disciplined. Tracy accepted his behavior. She let him go crazy!

Then she phoned me again. "I dunno what's gonna happen. Let me work on Star."

Two weeks later, I heard from Tracy again.

"Your contract won't be renewed, but I'll pay out your current one." Like her offer was a big deal . . . my current contract expired in one month.

"I have an idea. Think of something you can do around the station to make yourself useful."

Bitch, you put me up to doing this job. Then you switch control in midstream and give the power to Star?

I panicked. It was pandemonium. And at the same time, Bernard wasn't providing me with a shoulder to cry on. Bernard ignored me and zoned out on the PlayStation for hours on end. He ran the streets, taking midnight rides. I realized he had no depth . . . a bunch of dreams but no tools to achieve them. I had no one to lean on except his mother. "You are too good for my son," she said repeatedly. "You're bright. And as much as you want something for somebody, you can't make them be what they're not."

My sister Audrey advised, "Get a lawyer and start putting your audition tape together." Though initially interested in me, a rival station, Power 105.1, decided in the eleventh hour not to move forward because they knew that HOT 97 would start a legal battle due to my noncompete agreement.

Sharon, my pit-bull attorney, walked me into Tracy's office. Tracy again refused to negotiate with my legal counsel. "Who is this? I'm not gonna talk in front of her."

"I can do a gossip segment during Angie's show," I said, while Sharon waited in the lobby.

"That's a good idea," Tracy said, yet later she continued, "That wouldn't be fair to cut an hour off of Angie's show."

"Let's look at this way: Angie gets two weeks vacation; Sunny is going to need two weeks vacation. If you do some fill-ins on the weekends, that's $30,000 right there," Tracy said, her fingers gliding over her calculator.

She must be crazy. Sittin' around all available for when and if they call. Hell no!

At the same time, Wendy Williams, who was now at WBLS-FM, went on the air and kicked my back in. "Everybody, it's official! The Wendy Williams wannabe just got fired! Star is going to be looking for a new girl on Monday." It wasn't yet official that I was off the show. Deals were still being negotiated. But now the promoters of my gigs were calling to cancel, because my value to them lay in my ability to shout out their clubs on the air during the week.

Dropped like a hot potato.

Bentley offered me a spot to do gossip on his syndicated show "The All Star Mix Party," for $1,000 a week, which was beautiful. Now I knew I'd be okay. And I'd have a little bit of swagger with Tracy and not have to ass-kiss her.

Which way is up?

For two weeks, I removed myself from the world. I didn't go out. Or wash or comb my hair. No one from HOT 97 called me. I updated Bentley that I needed another day to get my mind right. To make matters worse, I sensed that there was something going on with Bernard and one of his side chicks.

My friend Charisse advised, "If you check his pager or his two-way, you'll find out about him, 'cause he's too sneaky for me." Sure enough, on the pager I had given him, I read the text messages between him and his side chick. And it was clear that their relationship was much more than he was telling me. Needing to hear the truth, and knowing that Bernard would continue with lies, I paged her. When she returned my page, she told me that she had been with him for a while.

Oh, okay. It's on.

Underneath my fury, my heart hurt like hell. And I wanted him to feel like I did.

Like a scene out of *Waiting to Exhale,* I rummaged through his belongings while he slept. The only difference was, I didn't set a bonfire.

When I checked his coat, a videotape was hidden in one of his pockets. Watching it in my VCR, the tape showed him touring a newly constructed house. "And this is going to be the living room, my daughter's room," he told whomever was holding the camera. As the camera zoomed out, I saw my truck in the background.

This muthafucka didn't pay rent and saved his $4,000 monthly disability checks to buy a damn house—to live in with some other bitch? This muthafucka done built a house behind my back.

Hot lava flowed out of my ears.

woke up Bernard's broke ass. "Get up and leave. Now!"

"Whatchu talkin' 'bout?" he said, looking up at me, wiping sleep from his eyes.

"I know about your side bitch! I know!"

Bernard refused to leave. Until I showed him the knife.

Yes. The knife. I don't need this shit.

"You have five seconds to leave my house!" We struggled. With me screaming and yelling, and tears streaming down my face. Bernard knocked me to the floor. He took the keys and left in my truck. I immediately filed a police report so the tracking device could be activated. His mother and sister denied knowing his whereabouts. Finally, my girlfriend and I found my truck parked in front of the side bitch's house.

"Bernard will be arrested if he doesn't return my truck," I told his mother from my cell phone.

Minutes later, his mother phoned back. "Bernard said he wants his things out of the house."

"Fine," I said, and watched him leave his baby mother's house. When he got into the truck and drove away, the police pulled him right over and arrested his ass. At the precinct, I showed the police the bruise on my arm from a fight with Bernard days earlier. Photos were taken. And two police detectives rearrested him. This time it was for his assault on me.

Weeks later, Bernard was still trying to hang around, stay in touch, work it all out . . . because he knew that an $18,000 check from FUBU was coming.

But I knew it too.

The day the check came, I left Bernard a message. And with lightning speed, he returned the call, trying to act like the $18,000 was the last thing on his mind. But when I knew he was coming, I stopped answering my telephone.

He called about forty times, asking the message machine, "What's wrong?"

When I finally answered, I said, "You know what's wrong! The jig is up. You said it was over between you and that bitch. And that was a lie. And by the way, I'm not giving you no fucking money!"

He broke.

"You never were going to give me no fucking money no way; that's why I hate you. You make me sick!"

It was all about money. God made it very clear and had been showing me all along. Throw some money in the picture, you'll see who the nigga is. When I look back on that relationship, I realize that I continued it not out of some illusion that it was a healthy one, but because I got caught up in the wedding season amongst my girlfriends. Everyone was getting married, except me. And as isolated as I was feeling working with Star, receiving zero support from Tracy, I wanted a man who would love and protect me.

Bernard taught me not to waste my time and not to ignore the signs.

I later learned that he had carried my photo around in his wallet years before he met me, telling people he was my boyfriend.

Wendy continued talking mad shit about me. My friend Daria, who also knows Wendy, phoned from California. I told her what was going on.

"And Wendy is on the radio talking about I'm a Wendy Williams wannabe, and to top it off, my father is dying." Daria called Wendy and gave her a piece of her mind. I was grateful for Daria's support.

"Wendy, do you know that Jonesy's father is dying? She just broke up with her boyfriend and her father is dying. And you know she's off the show and she doesn't know how she's going to pay the rent. This is not a game, Wendy!!" Daria told her.

That afternoon, Wendy called and apologized.

"Jones! It's Wendy! Are you all right? How's your father doing? What happened with your boyfriend? I had no idea. What are you going to do?" she asked in a low, throaty voice. I mumbled an answer.

"All right, listen, this is what you're gonna do. You're gonna call WPHI-FM in Philly and ask for Luscious Ice. You're gonna tell him that Wendy told you that they have a slot open and that I recommend you highly for it. If they need to call me for a reference, I'll vouch for you. And you're gonna do the same thing at my old station, Power 99. Send your CD to Golden Boy and you call me back when you mail it out. And I'll follow up."

Though she had viewed me as a competitor, I was surprised but then appreciated Wendy's unexpected generosity. I hoped that this was the beginning of building mutual support between us. I sent my air check and materials, as Wendy suggested. Though Golden Boy didn't respond, WPHI-FM did. In the meantime, I was being considered at a Connecticut radio station. Over the next four months, working with Bentley on his syndicated show kept me in radio and paid my bills. And I'd gotten Bernard flushed out of my system. Philadelphia was a place I had never considered working, but WPHI-FM later came back with an intriguing offer.

"We'll blow out our current morning show and give Miss Jones top salary if she'll agree to do mornings."

I was pissed at my lawyer. "I told you I didn't want mornings again, 'cause I can't deliver. It's too early."

"I think it's a great opportunity. You sound fantastic in the mornings. You have a chance to build your own show. And they're willing to support you with billboards or whatever."

What am I thinking? I'm trying to be picky?

I accepted the offer.

My sister Audrey had advised that I take Philly, since it was the number-four market, as opposed to Connecticut, which was the fifty-third market. Market rankings are determined by the amount of listeners. WBLS-FM's program director, Vinny Brown, expressed interest in hiring me. Worries about keeping a roof over my head now rolled off of my back. I was back in the game.

Toya Beasley, program director of KISS-FM, introduced me to their then-consultant Barry Mayo during a quick stop at the station. Over lunch, I confided all of what I had just experienced. "Wow! For you to trust me with that information means a lot to me. I'd love to be your mentor—I think you're very talented, and there's very little talent in radio."

The sun peeked from behind a dark cloud.

On the morning of my birthday, Tracy called and asked that I fill in for Angie. My contract with WPHI-FM in Philly wasn't beginning for another two weeks. "If you do it, I'll pay double time. And we can get you a cake or somethin'."

But during the shift, Tracy barked, "Do we have to hear that it's your birthday all day?! Listeners don't care that it's your birthday."

Tracy was still being a bitch.

While I was on the air, an emergency meeting was called in the station conference room. When it was over, Tracy came into the studio, where I was ending a conversation with a listener. Tracy's face was more pale than usual. "Judy Ellis announced her resignation. Don't worry; as long as I got my job, you guys' jobs are safe," Tracy said. My board operator and whoever else was in there shared their concerns about their status.

Whateva! Bitch, I don't give a fuck. Besides I'm not even here but one night a week. I'm only filling in. Remember, you fired me. That's what y'all bitches get.

If Judy had handed in her resignation in the middle of the afternoon, that meant she'd been fired. And I'm glad I was there to see the hurt and the worry in both Judy's and Tracy's eyes when I passed them in the hallway. Maybe they would learn about the hurt they've caused other people.

Tracy didn't pay me double time as she had promised. "No, Jonesy, I didn't make that promise," she said.

"Okay, fine, Tracy." Unbeknownst to her, my deal with WPHI-FM was inked. The contract had been signed. And I would launch my own morning show on November 24th.

I felt great. Bernard was out of my hair. Powerful mentors and friends sincerely cared about my life and wanted to see me succeed. And Judy was out.

God put me here to see the chaos. And I felt vindicated.

I was doing Angie's Sunday-night show. The studio telephone rang.

"Yo, I just wanna congratulate you, 'cause of all of the obstacles that you went through and you're still holding your head up. I heard that you're getting ready to go to Philly. That's a good look for you. I wanted to know what you're doing on a management level." It was Kevin, Wendy Williams's husband.

Silence.

"Big Phil is my manager. So you need to talk to him."

"Big Phil? That's my man!" Big Phil was the manager that promoters had to go through to book me to host their parties. He was really in my corner during this whole time and told me to keep my focus and that everything was going to work out.

"Wendy already did Philly, so you might need some help to walk you through doors. And that nigga Colby you're about to work for in Philly, he's a snake. He was a snake with Wendy."

"Uh-huh."

"So when are you going to Philly?"

"Tonight, after my show."

"You're gonna drive all of the way to Philly tonight?" It was around 9:00 P.M. "Well, let's hook up for dinner before y'all ride out."

Kevin, Big Phil and I met up at a restaurant in Midtown Manhattan. Kevin made his proposal to represent me. And Wendy called in for updates from Kevin, wanting to know what I was saying.

Kevin thought I would be impressed with his sales pitch: "There are a lot of offers coming Wendy's way, but she won't be able to do them all. So we can pass on the extra to you." Big Phil and I decided to give Kevin a try, but not to sign a contract. During the drive to Philly, Big Phil and I talked about my future, and the turmoil that had just occurred.

"You'll be back," he said. "And when you are, that's gonna be your morning show. That nigga Star is going to be sick. Watch!"

That next morning, Kevin, Big Phil and I met in the lobby of WPHI-FM. And when Philadelphia's WPHI-FM program director, Colby Colb, turned the corner and saw Kevin, he turned as pale as a black man could.

TWELVE

I'M HERE TO CHILL IN PHILLY

Jonesy's Juice:

Judge Greg Mathis: Judge Mathis reminds me of my uncles. Underneath his charming, corporate smile lurks a Detroit playa ready for a street fight. When he sits behind the microphone, Judge Mathis brings it. He knows that he has a limited amount of time to inform and throw in a few chuckles. And he doesn't take any shit, and will come back on you so fast, you wonder what happened to the kindly judge. He cursed out Wendy Williams when she tried to play him out by asking him about being on drugs. "What? I know you're not talking. I'll tear this whole muthafuckin' studio up and you can get your man. 'Cause we can handle this right here and right now," he said.

By letting Wendy know that she had him confused with some chump, Judge Mathis carried order in her court. I love that man!

"**I ain't no ugly** nigga!"

"I never said that you were, but you're married and I don't fuck with married men."

This conversation was just one of the "Welcome to Philly" greetings I encountered as an entrée to Philadelphia's exclusive celebrity scene. But instead of a reception from Philadelphia Mayor John Street, I had to banter with the other ruler of the city, then Philadelphia 76er Allen Iverson.

The Philly elite scene is small and cliquish, with exclusive soirees that take place in the homes of athletes and entertainers. Unlike in New York City, where you might party with P Diddy at Marquee, or Beyoncé may be next in line for your bathroom stall at Jay-Z's 40/40 Club, Philly celebrities like to keep their lives sequestered from average folks. Occasionally, the rich and famous would invite interlopers to take part in their fast circle in exchange for keeping their mouths shut. In other words, you never repeated what you saw or whom you knew. And if you were invited to partake in sexual dalliances, just know what you are doing and what you signed up for. Don't come crying the "victim" song later, because nobody is trying to hear that. Like in every city, there are women who are dying to be passed around by a circle of athletes, all for the glory of having boasting rights on what athlete they slept with.

I tried to downplay the history I was making in this black music Mecca as the first African-American female morning host at 103.9 The Beat. Philadelphia was number six in the national market, and my show was fourth in the ratings. Nothing but real musicians in Philly: The Sounds of Philadelphia, Gamble and Huff, Teddy Pendergrass, Patti LaBelle, Jill Scott, Eve, and others. The depth of music emerging from the City of Brotherly Love easily rivaled that of New York City.

Wendy's husband, Kevin Hunter, never became my manager. He accompanied Big Phil and me for the ride and made sure that what management had agreed to was abided. Though he eagerly wanted me to sign a contract, I never trusted nor wanted Kevin to represent my business interests, because of the "Wendy wannabe" comments his wife had made after my ousting from HOT 97. Plus, I felt that Kevin's hot head could affect my business interests negatively.

When Kevin realized that I wasn't going to sign his contract, he said, "You know, you're full of shit. I'm not wasting my time." Kevin assumed that I would be impressed by getting Wendy's leftover offers.

I would be less than honest if I didn't admit that when the on-air red light came on in November 2002, I was nervous. Without fanfare, I focused on developing content for the program, forming a bond with my new cohosts, and perfecting my on-air character. My role then, and now, is to entertain—to create the kind of show that listeners talk about, long after we're off of the air. Up until this time, my role was always that of a sidekick, the female voice, or a part-timer, but this show had my name on it: *Jonesy in the Morning*. I was hired to be the captain of the ship, and for the first time in Philadelphia radio, a female voice, my voice, would not have to giggle to a male host's feeble attempts at jokes. I would no longer have to represent only female listeners. And, thank God, I no longer had to ask for permission to speak. It was a daring move, which probably startled Philly listeners at first—hearing a woman voicing her opinion unapologetically, without a concern on who agreed with her opinions on politics, gossip or the traffic on the Schuylkill Expressway. If anyone had a problem with my viewpoint, that was fine but I expressed no fear and never backed down. It was time for a female broadcaster who never kissed the ass of celebrity guests or those in power and gave the listeners the unfiltered truth instead of some publicist-generated bullshit. It was time that *Jonesy in the Morning* set a strong precedent in radio. All the departments of WPHI-FM loved the concept and supported the show, including the Program Director/Afternoon Drive host Colby Colb and the sales-and-promotions staff, which placed billboards featuring the show from Mount Airy to Chester. I lobbied and was able to include DJ Bent Roc as producer for the show over Colby's objections; Colby claimed that he had never heard of Bent. Because I needed a seasoned team around me, I made it clear, "If Bent isn't hired, you're going to have a problem with me." Colby later gave Bent a Saturday night shift and sang his praises after his wife expressed love for Bent's show. On the day the Arbitron rating spring book was released, my newsperson, Sherry Lee Stevens, and I ran to her office to learn our standing. Arbitron is a research company that collects data on the listening habits of radio audiences. Their data is sold to advertisers, who then determine how much money is spent with a given program at a radio station.

Jonesy in the Morning had climbed the ratings chart from fourteenth to fourth place in three months. Jay Black, Bent Roc and Sherry Lee were excited that they were on a successful show. The character I had created had connected with listeners. For the first time in urban radio history in a top market, there was a fearless broadcaster holding the powerfuls' feet to the fire. Celebrities, politicians and anyone peddling their viewpoints or a new movie before my listeners weren't permitted to dance around issues. I didn't permit free kiss-ass publicity for those who wanted to sell their wares, rip off the community and keep on stepping. No one was allowed to float publicist bullshit and not be called on the carpet. And millions of listeners ate it up. Listeners that had been loyal to competitor Power 99 had made the switch and were now listening to my show. My friend and colleague Bent Roc was now thrilled he had come to Philly from New York. It probably was shocking at first to hear a young black woman speak the swagger that only male broadcasters had been expected to get away with. But soon the City of Brotherly Love knew that if there was something to be said, Miss Jones would rock the morning and expose what everyone was thinking anyway. Doug heard about my success and phoned to offer congratulations. The conversation was friendly and inspiring. He gave praise where praise was due. And we both appreciated the opportunity that life presented for us to be friends again.

Doug promised to perform in my honor at an upcoming celebration party.

Power 99 hired Lisa "Golden Girl" Natson in response, because as Doc Wynter, a Clear Channel manager, said, "You proved that female-led programs are lucrative and a viable option for broadcast companies. But for you, Golden Girl would not have ever gotten the opportunity." However, General Manager Lynn Bruder didn't share our joy. She was more upset that our sister rock station Y100 had done horribly, even though they had a skilled producer in Rick Delgado on board.

A fabulous number-four party was thrown at an upscale downtown restaurant in my honor by station management, and the finest of Philly—whoever was not on tour or locked up—were among the well-wishers who wanted to get their dance on with headliners Doug E. Fresh and Big Daddy Kane.

As I headed for the celebration, I phoned Doug from my limo to see how close he was.

"Huh? Tarsha, you never got back to me. Remember, I asked you who was promoting it? 'Cause to do something for you for free is one thing, but for niggas charging money, they got to pay."

I had been bragging on-air about my best friend Doug E. Fresh, and now I had to find a way to save face. Big Daddy Kane fulfilled his promise, and became the headliner, tearing down the house. For the first time I met sponsors and advertisers and their spouses. I was puzzled that throughout the evening, with sponsors and management I had to dispel the perception that Colby Colb had recruited me from New York. It was annoying that Colby had taken to openly bragging that he'd hired me, which was the furthest thing from the truth.

"**H**ow you lettin' this New Yorker in? We from Philly. Philly doing Philly. Everybody know Jonesy gets on from laying down with the boxers," snarled Lisa "Golden Girl" Natson to her listeners.

ormer Syracuse University classmate and Detroit Pis-
ton Derrick Coleman was now a Philadelphia 76er. Derrick was very protective of me and made sure that I could call him
anytime. I've always appreciated our friendship, because Derrick
never changed his personality as he became successful in the NBA.
And no matter the distance or time between us, he and I always re-
sumed where we had left off, making sure to invite each other to important milestones in our lives, such as his New Jersey wedding.
Derrick wanted me to move into his building, but it's rent was more
too expensive. Eventually, he helped me find Lincoln Greene, a gated
apartment complex, where visitors had to be buzzed in.

Leaving all of my friends in New York City, and with family living in various cities, I set about creating a new social life. I knew no
one in Philadelphia except Derrick Coleman, who traveled often
during the season, and was new to Philly also, and just settling into
his own new digs. Later I fought for Bentley to join my morning
show, so there was at least one more friendly face from my past with
me. In order to meet the listeners, I created Grown Folk Fridays,
a weekly party that was anchored at the trendy Pegasus nightclub.
Partygoers enjoyed rotating DJs and drink specials. The party was
heavily promoted by the radio station and quickly became the place
to be in Philadelphia. It became the rare Philly event that attracted
people of all walks of life. Local celebrities like DJ Jazzy Jeff frequently came through to hang out. Attending Sixer games was my
favorite pastime, and when I blew up on WPHI, the Sixer organization invited me to sing the national anthem. I had done a tour of the
majority of the basketball arenas to sing the national anthem, so this
was not a new experience, and it was one that I enjoyed.

One evening, not long after *Jonesy in the Morning* increased in the
ratings, some of the Philadelphia Sixers came to my Grown Folk Fridays night.

"I like your show a lot," then-Sixer Aaron McKee said, after introducing himself. His teammate Allen Iverson was sending me seductive eye messages, which I ignored. Eventually, Iverson gave up and told my friend Charisse to bring me over to him, as if the king couldn't bear to rise from his throne. Later, after chatting briefly and forming our own little party, Iverson and his crew showed up at my apartment complex. The starstruck security guard buzzed in Iverson, who began circling the complex, yelling my name in the dark of night, disturbing the neighbors. After I guided him to the apartment from my balcony, Iverson did a territorial stroll and walked straight into my bedroom and lay across my bed, as if it were his house. Charisse and I looked at him like he was a silly boy and left him alone in the bedroom, returning to the living room, making small talk.

"Come in here. I want to talk to you," Iverson came out and said, after getting tired of being by himself in my bedroom. When I walked into my bedroom, he kept trying to push up, seeing if he could convince me into letting him have his sexual way with me. He must have gotten me confused with the low-self-esteem groupies he was used to dealing with. Finally, after an hour and a half of badgering, Iverson gave up and asked, "Can I just lay down my head for a minute?" Eventually, he gave up and left. No slam-dunk booty for him.

Iverson and I became great friends. I grew to understand him because Philly gave him a hard time for many years. He didn't understand why he was so criticized for what he did off the court, when he more than sacrificed and contributed his body for the game. Iverson has a career average of 30.6 points, 4.2 rebounds, 6.1 assists and 2.19 steals in sixty-two playoff games. What else did Philadelphia want from the man? Being friends with Iverson was like being in college, where there is a perception that there are no responsibilities and no one to answer to. With him, you were always in search of the next thrill, no matter how wild the scheme.

"Hey! What you doing?" AI was on the other end of the phone, the

ringing of which had woken me up. I looked over at the alarm clock—
it blinked 5:15 A.M.

"Getting ready to leave for work, like I do every morning."

"Call off of work, I'll pay today's salary."

"I can't call off of work like that."

"Why not? It's just a day. Come on. We getting ready to drive up to
New York. Come hang out with us."

In Iverson's universe, everyone was on standby to come out and play
with him, and Philadelphia was his playground. If he saw the New
York plates on my truck traveling the opposite direction, he would follow, block me off, and would laughingly climb into the driver's seat
and sit on top of me, just to amuse himself. Iverson would have me hol-
lering so loud, passersby didn't know whether to phone for help or request his autograph.

Meanwhile, Aaron McKee would phone occasionally and invite
me to his barbecues. But he retreated when AI made advances toward me. Every basketball team has a pecking order among the players. And the star gets first choice on anything, including women; this
policy holds true whether or not the star is married. The more AI
and I became friends, the more Aaron McKee backed off. Players
never wanted to have a confrontation with AI. What Iverson wants,
Iverson gets, even though I wasn't interested in a relationship beyond
friendship.

"Jonesy showed me a photo of her beautiful home and I'm going to
bless the kitchen and cook for you." Superstar and matchmaker Patti
LaBelle co-signed me on the air to a thrilled listening audience. Patti is
a phenomenal woman. Despite the tragedies she has endured, she always gives her time and her heart when I need her. When she glided
into the studio at 8:00 A.M. wearing full makeup, a red designer pant-
suit and stiletto heels, she whispered like a playful aunt, "I be listening
to you. You give people the business." Patti LaBelle is the truth when it
comes to longevity in entertainment. While some up-and-coming artists

refuse to do morning radio, Patti continues to be available to her legions of fans.

Miss Patti has always known my heart. She listened patiently and shared my joy as I told her, like a little girl on Christmas Day, about purchasing my dream home. It was at the end of a cul-de-sac, with floor-to-ceiling windows and nine-foot ceilings. The walls were built of stone from the Colorado mountains, and the stone also framed the fireplace and adorned a sunken living room. There was a separate dining room, with built-in cabinetry; a wraparound full-sized deck outside the kitchen; a sunroom and a master bedroom. There were two additional huge bedrooms, with walk-in closets and a Jacuzzi, which made the house the perfect bachelorette home for entertaining. The two bedrooms on the second floor with built-in twin beds were perfect for my visiting nephews.

"**W**hat's up with you and my son? Why don't you go out with Zuri?" Patti asked more than once. I had met Zuri and his business partner, Dr. J's son, after one of their charity parties. We soon began having long telephone conversations and occasional lunches. Though there wasn't any "love" chemistry, Zuri and I maintained a supportive friendship and I was always included in their family functions. During one of Zuri's birthday parties, Miss Patti and I danced so hard that I fractured my foot and had to wear it wrapped for weeks.

"SURPRISE," the star-studded crowd yelled to a floored Miss Patti as her high heels slowly clicked across her marble foyer and she stared into every gleaming face. Seconds earlier, she'd complained, not knowing that a mouthwatering buffet and a houseful of loving friends awaited her, "Did y'all cook some dinner? 'Cause I'm hungry."

"**J**onesy! Come here, girl!" I loved how she always embraced me like a long-lost daughter. Patti guided me through her spacious, well-adorned home to the private area where her concert costumes, trophies and awards were displayed, while everyone, including Turquoise Irving, Dr. J.'s wife, danced around the moonlit swimming pool to Stevie Wonder's "Happy Birthday" song. Not wearing what she wanted, Patti changed into a new ensemble, laid out by her wardrobe person, and returned to the dance area, where she asked the DJ to play 50 Cent's "In da Club." And despite claims that she was too tired to sing, Miss Patti blew a beautiful rendition of "Over the Rainbow" that woke birds as far south as the Mason-Dixon line.

One morning, after interviewing recording artist Jill Scott, whose confidence I loved but I thought she was a little snooty for a fat girl, a breaking story came over the Associated Press wires. The Philadelphia police needed help to solve the murder of an Asian man from the Strawberry Mansion section of the city who was trying to protect his son from getting his bicycle stolen. So far there had been no leads and no witnesses, which enraged me. I knew that someone had to have seen something, especially in that neighborhood, where there was always somebody sitting in the window, being nosy, and watching somebody do something. That day, through four commercial breaks, I cried out to the listeners, "That could have been you or your child! If you saw something, anything, let the police know. It would be a shame if the little boy grew up and never knew the punk who murdered his father." Sure enough, later that afternoon, one of my listeners called the police. The tip led the cops to arrest the slimy perpetrator. As a result, I was honored with the City of Philadelphia's Hero Award. The public acclaim that I received in Philadelphia helped to put my professional and personal woes behind me. I really hoped that a period of happiness was headed my way.

"What's up? Whatchu doing?" It was Zuri, phoning to invite me to another gathering at his family's home.

"I'm on my way to New York to identify my father's body. The doctors tried three times to resuscitate him, but now he's gone. And my sisters live too far away, so I have to go."

"You're by yourself? Who's with you? Omigod, I am so sorry. Why didn't you call me?" I cried an ocean of tears through Zuri's questions. I don't know if I ever answered him. I somehow managed to get dressed for the long drive to Jersey City to identify my father's body. It's extremely uncomfortable to identify a loved one's body, as if all that they created resulted only in a limp physical form. Audrey and Marcia phoned me earlier, on a conference call, and we argued whether the doctors should resuscitate Billy again. As the bitching continued, with everybody asserting their opinions, the hospital interrupted the argument once and for all. "We're sorry to inform you that your father has passed away."

Billy had been paralyzed for years from alcoholism. My cousin Rhonda, who still lived in the same house as my father, also drank a lot. During one of their frequent arguments, Rhonda pushed my father down the stairs and broke his arm. Billy hated hospitals and lost use of his arm, letting it heal like a chicken wing. Subsequently, he had a stroke and couldn't talk, using his eyes to communicate with his home health-care attendant. When my sisters and I visited him during periodic hospital stays, he still had his fire and would either anger us or make us laugh. Rhonda used Billy to vent all the rage she felt while she was pregnant with twins. One twin died and the other was born mentally retarded.

Seeing the hell that Rhonda and Billy were determined to live with, I stopped going to Jersey City as frequently. I never felt guilty because they knew they were drinking themselves into a grave. Now I had to throw my shit on and drive to Jersey from Philly, at midnight.

My last parent was gone. First Sonny, then my mother, now Billy. Though he and I never had a traditional father-daughter relationship, I regretted that we didn't communicate more. I may never understand the effect of having distant relationships with both fathers. But I do think that fatherlessness has a negative impact on not only little boys, but girls too. Some would say that you cannot miss what you never had, but I disagree. Every child, whether they admit it or not, wants to have the opportunity to connect with their parents. During my early years I probably wouldn't have had the wisdom to know it.

"Jonesy, it's Miss Pat. Listen, I just want you to know that I love you. Zuri loves you. And whether it be a friend, a mother or a sister that you need and you want to talk, please don't hesitate to call me. I'm doing the Mann Music Center tonight, but I'll be home by 10:00 P.M. And I don't care how late it is—if you need to talk, you give me a call. All right? Because I love you and you are going to get through this." Patti was kind enough to leave this touching sentiment on my voice mail. I really needed to hear it, and combined with the support that I received from my sisters, bosses and coworkers, I was able to get through that time. Having lost three sisters to cancer at relatively young ages, Patti instinctively knew what I was feeling. When they made their transition, my mother was forty-seven years old, Sonny was fifty-four, and Billy was fifty-nine.

Beanie Sigel, a rapper on the Roc-A-Fella label, had come on my show and was mad because I demanded that both sides be presented in his first attempted-murder trial. He had been charged with attempted murder and reckless endangerment for nearly shooting to death a man on a crowded street in Philadelphia. Occasionally, a celebrity would test me, thinking that just because we were on friendly terms they could own my microphone. Beanie soon learned that wasn't the case. My listeners deserved to hear representatives from both sides. And they did. I invited the attorney for the defense to the show. To this day, Beanie still has a problem with me over that.

Oh, well.

I actually felt great not being in a relationship. That is, after I successfully mourned my relationships with Doug, Bryant, and Bernard, I was able to release my anger toward them and put the relationships in context, taking responsibility for whatever drama I brought to the table. An unhealthy emotional pattern had occurred with these men. And I chose to ignore the early signs, but whatever I was aware of, I didn't have the tools then to get what I needed or separate myself from each man. We'd had meaningful conversations about everything except what really mattered to me—loyalty and commitment.

Fortunately, these relationships were a catalyst to teach me how to be happy and alone. Go to the movies alone. Go to a restaurant and have a great meal alone. Find activities that I didn't even know I enjoyed, such as plays, magic shows—alone. Browse through a bookstore, and read anything that piqued my interest—alone. Earlier in my life, especially in my relationship with Walter, my own health or physical safety was never a priority. I didn't value my health. With Doug, I got into my fitness and began to get yearly physicals and pamper myself with regular massages. Never before had I taken an interest in my own self-care.

And once I was away from both of them, and released other toxic relationships, I was able to create a whole new career—by myself—and I spread my wings.

Now I was going out, meeting people, and had formed Jonesy and the Pussycats, which contributed to organizations such as the Clothing Drive for Returning Women to the Workforce. I also formed a book club, which met monthly, often featuring local authors in an intimate setting. Everything was great professionally, but with no one man in my life, I lacked male companionship.

I was recovering from my fractured foot during one of my Grown Folk Fridays parties. Resting at the bar, I chatted with passersby at Pegasus. A dark brother with a bald head and long eyelashes and a stocky football-player build compared me with the promotional photo on the wall. Other men strolled by, giving double takes when they recognized me. This particular guy introduced himself as "Shaun," sharing little information about himself. His sarcastic swagger and animated personality attracted me.

"We need to cut through all of the bullshit, so give me your number now." That was Shaun's way of romancing me. And it worked, because we exchanged telephone numbers. When I phoned him a few days later, he accused me of giving him the wrong telephone number.

"I was like, 'the bitch gave me the wrong number and played me out, and I wanted to hook up with her.' "

"You had the right number, you just dialed the wrong digits. Anyway, I see on your business card that you're a photographer. I need your info—your name, address and Social Security—so I can tell my friend Bentley where I'm going, since I'm in a new town and will be with a virtual stranger."

Our first date was at a barbecue at the home of Shaun's close friend. When he opened my car door, Shaun said, "Don't get used to this, I'm only opening the door because it's the first date." People recognized me at the barbeque and began asking for autographs, but when the crowd melted away, Shaun was nowhere to be found. When I located him, I asked, "Why'd you leave me?"

" 'Cause I saw you signing autographs and acting like you weren't with me."

As we got to know each other, Shaun felt familiar—as the cliché goes, like I had known him my entire life.

We spent most of our time together at his South Jersey home, where Shaun would cook delicious dinners and surprise me with a bottle of champagne. Like kids, we would escape to Great Adventure, often doubling with Charisse and her date. "Wow!" Charisse said. "Jonesy got a boyfriend. He acts like he's really feeling you!" It felt like a warm blanket to have a man's arm around me who I could share my heart with and to confess the trials and tribulations of my professional life.

"**W**e have to take you off the air." After the morning show, human resources director Steven Golsch summoned me to his office. Representatives of Whitney Houston were threatening to sue the radio station for a report I had broadcasted three days earlier about an allegation that mentioned possible abuse of their daughter, Bobbi Kristina. I had flashbacks of Whitney's telephone call to my home when I was at HOT 97. Cathy Hughes, the founder and CEO of Radio One, of which WPHI was an affiliate, had heard about the controversy and was upset because Whitney was about to sign a promotional deal with Radio One. And now, because of my comments, Whitney was threatening to not go forward with it.

"For how long?"

"Right now we don't know, we're going to see how things go, wait until they calm down. You need to be mindful of what you say."

"Well, you don't mind when what I say brings up the ratings."

"The station will report that you're on vacation."

My name was always in the Philadelphia newspapers, either for a community-service acknowledgment or a controversy I created or was alleged to have created. I had just placed a deposit on a house in Conshohocken, and I was afraid that I would lose a career that I loved. When negative controversy appeared, Program Director Colby Colb would behave as if he suddenly didn't understand the morning show's concept. When revenues increased and we continued to climb in the ratings, he was thrilled. But when a situation occurred that would threaten his livelihood, Colby was quick to attack me.

The media had a field day reporting on the Whitney controversy. The *Philadelphia Daily News* wrote, "103.9 The Beat DJ Jonesy is under heat by Whitney Houston and her lawyers after a comment on her 'Jonesy in the A.M.' show. Houston's attorney, Marty Singer, said Tuesday, 'A claim has been made over comments [by Jonesy] about Whitney Houston's family.' Jonesy hasn't been on-air since July 10.

The station says she's on vacation. A source at 103.9 FM tells the *Daily News* that the remarks concerning Houston's daughter and Houston's brother were referencing a story that a tabloid was writing on the singer."

"I got to get you out of the house. Stop worrying. Whatever happens will happen," Shaun said, trying to console me. He was right. My future was out of my hands. The decision on whether I returned to helm *Jonesy in the Morning* rested with management, and I was not entirely confident that they were in my corner.

Atlantic City became my hideout. I still appeared at Grown Folk Fridays, and waited and worried while the deliberations continued. My personal lawyer soon revealed his disloyalty: "If you hadn't opened your big mouth, we wouldn't be in this position now."

"And if it weren't for the comments I made, you wouldn't have a job right now, would you?" The sharks were circling and I was unclear as to where the next blow would come from. On a daily basis, I had to get my nasty bastard lawyer to give me updates. It was my idea that he should try to take meetings with Whitney's people.

Driving to Great Adventure with Shaun, he switched the station from The Beat, to Power 99, which aired a Golden Girl promo that raked me over the coals. "Can you believe that she would stoop that low? And all of it for ratings. I been trying to tell y'all not to like her." This chick had decided to use my turmoil to add a few notches on her neophyte radio belt, instead of developing fresh, original content for her show or minding her own damn business.

Shaun said harshly, "She's killing you! And you can't do nothin' about it! You have no voice! They took your voice from you!"

"You're supposed to be my friend?" I asked. We hadn't been dating that long, but his opinions bothered me. He didn't bother to defend me or turn off the radio.

"I'm just playing! I know you're gonna land on your feet. You're the one who's worried." Though Shaun pretended that his comments were jokes, it was obvious that he couldn't process the seriousness of my situation. I would be in legal, professional and financial trouble if Whitney Houston pursued a case against the radio station and me. I wasn't able to let go of his comments. They echoed the disloyalty I'd experienced with Bernard.

I received a threatening voice-mail message from a familiar voice. "Yeah, I hear you're in Philly, stealing my style. I don't wanna have to come for you, because I'm about to be on in Philly and other markets, so I don't wanna have to come for you, but I will."

It was Star, aka Troi Torain.

Eventually, Whitney's feathers were smoothed, and after two weeks, I returned to the airwaves without fanfare. I apologized for the Whitney incident so early in the morning that no one heard it. Since my abrupt "vacation," the radio station had lost so many listeners that our audience didn't know when I was returning. But once the station aired promo spots that *Jonesy in the Morning* was back, station management were ecstatic, counting the bounced-back revenue.

"**T**arsha, Rhonda passed away this morning." When I heard the news, I phoned Audrey from a radio-station promotion in Jamaica. My coworkers and I had been on a whirlwind schedule, conducting interviews, hosting listener receptions and preparing for the next day's broadcast. It took more than a moment before my brain wrapped around the loss of Cousin Rhonda. My cousin who took me under her wing. Rhonda who loved me. That Rhonda. I pulled myself out a self-induced puddle, my coworkers throwing me worried glances. My sister said that Rhonda was found dead in her bed.

When I inquired about Rhonda's child, Audrey assured me that she had taken custody. That I shouldn't worry about coming home, because the living room was crowded with our five uncles and their families. Audrey knew that I never could have sat through Rhonda's funeral. After Billy's death, it was a pain that I couldn't revisit. And I knew that if anyone ever needed four protectors in a time of need, there were no better loyal fighters than my uncles Marvin, Bobby, Herbert and James. Along with my father, Billy, they're the type of men who though are in their fifties and sixties, have spent their entire lives ready to "set it off." Dapper on the outside. Straight gangster on the inside. No need to phone the police when they're around. They will become the judge, jury and your correction officer and funeral director if you mess with someone they love. No questions asked.

Once, when Rhonda's girlfriend and husband refused to return her van, one uncle calmly said, "Say that your uncles are coming to get the van. They can do one of two things: They can bring the van right now or we can go get the van." The van was returned within the hour. I love the strength of my uncles. Though our family has had its battles, those men have always made me feel protected.

Two months later, I was pregnant.
   "When was the last time you had your period? Wake up! When did you last have your period?"
   "What?" It was two o'clock in the morning. Four hours before I had to be at work. My memory was groggy. I thought I was dreaming when Shaun shook me out of my sleep.
   "Get up! We're going to the store." Sure enough, when we returned from the local pharmacy, the test results indicated that I was indeed pregnant. We both were stunned by Shaun's premonition.

"Tarsha!" Shaun kept calling me into my bathroom, where he was lounging in the bubble-filled Jacuzzi. Everytime I would come in, he would say, "Never mind."
   Finally I said, "Nigga, I am in here now. What do you want?"
   "Let's just do it. I want the whole thing. Kids. You. Fuck it, let's get married. Let's have a family." I knew this was supposed to be one of those tender moments that every little girl dreams of, but it

wasn't for me. Shaun had some insincere behavior about him, and deep down, I knew that I was not completely in love with him. Still, I said, "Yes," and accepted that this version of love was all life had to offer.

When I first met Shaun, he said, "I wanna wait three years before I marry anybody but I want to have a baby right now." And he knew that I wouldn't have a child outside of marriage. In fact, every man I have been with has known. But they've all proposed to improve whatever situation they were in or to move out of their mother's house. And to them, they thought I was the ticket to ride. During one previous comical proposal, I told an ex-boyfriend, Joseph, "Of course you wanna marry me. You wanna move out of your mother's house! You're forty-five and have no money and share a bank account with your mother."

Sometimes Shaun and I were able to move past harsh words and become excited over the birth of our baby. We communicated better and had times when we would run laughingly out of the house, often twice in one afternoon, shopping for baby products. Other times we would fight over stupid nonsense. As soon as I started planning a wedding, Shaun didn't want to be bothered.

When I told my coworkers, everyone hugged and congratulated me on my pregnancy, but I didn't talk about it on the air. That weekend I looked forward to daydreaming about the arrival of my baby.

That Saturday, returning from a maternity boutique in West Philly, I was stopped by a police officer. I hadn't been speeding and the intersection I'd just entered had a green traffic signal. The scowl on the face of the white cop as he approached my black Mercedes truck indicated that he had a point to prove.

"You people drive like that in New York, ah? Where the hell do you think you're going?"

"What the fuck do you mean by that?" I had missed the class that said I should be courteous to white racist cops. He thought I was just some drug dealer's bitch running some dope. He completed his bull-shit paperwork and tossed the trumped-up violations at me. Before I drove off, I said, "Be sure to listen to my show in the morning, 'cause you're about to get your fifteen minutes of fame."

During the seven o'clock, highly listened-to morning-drive hour, I gave the name, rank, and serial number of this cop, and talked about his ass for over an hour. Now I knew how black people who were voiceless felt, and I made it my business to let the Philadelphia Police Department know that I wasn't going to take their shit and be silent about it. It got to the point where the traffic cop's captain called to say that if I didn't stop talking about the incident, they would take other measures. When I continued, the cop's partner called and threatened me on the air: "We can make you disappear" was what millions of listeners heard that morning.

Soon after, a twelve-year-old girl phoned. We'd had a hilarious morning, peppered with lots of jokes and gags, but it was clear from the sadness in her voice that her reaching out was no joking matter. After a few moments to gather her courage, she revealed, "My mother's boyfriend has been touching me."

Stunned, I said, "Does your mother know?"

"Uh-huh, but my mother said to be patient until she could get paperwork for a new apartment." Outraged, I didn't know who to call first. Her mother, to curse her out? The police, to report a crime? Or my boys from New York, who knew how to step on punks who molest little girls? Despite my frying one of their colleagues, detectives came to the station to verify the authenticity of the call. Eventually, they located the caller, and despite the continuous denials of the mother, the beautiful young girl was removed from the home. Her voice still haunts me to this day. Not long after, I created a club for teenagers, where they could socialize in a wholesome environment.

In the meantime, David Chang, a Taiwanese-American, created a game called Ghettopoly. Based upon the classic Monopoly game, players draw "Hustle" and "Ghetto Stash" cards, with directions like "You're a little short on loot, so you decided to stick up a bank. Collect $75" and "Steal $$$ if you pass Let$ Roll." When the press release came into the studio, my jaw fell open. I was outraged, and promptly let my listeners know about this racist board game. On his website, David Chang was unapologetic and promised that more games— Hoodopoly, Hiphopopoly, Thugopoly and Redneckopoly—were coming soon. I urged, "Why don't we flip Chang's concept and make a racist game about Asians. We'll call it Chinkopoly. If you have any stereotypes, call in now." Tired of being the butt of jokes created by members of other ethnic groups, listeners jammed the switchboard with their own contributions. "Let them hear how it feels" was the popular sentiment.

The next day various Asian groups protested to General Manager Bruder, including the Asian American Journalists Association of Philadelphia, whose president, Murali Balaji, wrote, "[R]ather than looking at the across the board offensive nature of the game, Miss Jones, 'Jonesy in the A.M.,' chose to focus on how an Asian American could make a game about blacks and Latinos. She proceeded to create her own game, 'Chinkopoly,' urging callers to make degrading imitations of Asians and using old stereotypes as 'properties' for her game. We are strongly asking for a public on-air apology from Miss Jones and are likely to urge a boycott of Philly 103.9 if one is not issued immediately. We would also like the chance to have Miss Jones speak at a town-hall meeting we will set up specifically to address how the board game and Miss Jones' response to the game have heightened tensions among communities of color."

Bruder's response to me was, "Jonesy, would you mind calling her? I'm not telling or asking you to apologize, just let her vent so we can move on." Through the speakerphone in Bruder's office, I let Murali Balji have her say. But I could tell that it wasn't enough; she wanted an argument. And she got one:

"Yes, he was wrong, but you are making it worse," she said.

"Jonesy is here to listen and to reach an understanding," Bruder said, playing mediator.

"What are you doing to protest David Chang's actions?" There was silence. Baliji couldn't tell me what they were doing to affect his life. She knew that I had a valid point, but she also knew that her group was so used to marching and boycotts, they didn't have to acknowledge the pain of the black community over the creation and distribution of the Ghettopoly game, which had been on the market for at least a year. It was clear that the Asian American Journalists Association of Philadelphia had no problem with Ghettopoly until it was flipped on them.

"I don't care if Miss Jones is remorseful. We are going to take her actions to the next level."

"Bitch, I don't give a fuck." I disconnected the call.

Lynn Bruder shook her head and said, "You should have made her feel as if she had the last word."

"I don't do that," I replied. Balaji knew that I wasn't apologetic because I had not done anything more than stand up for black people who didn't have the power to lodge their complaints against racist images. And her allegations that I was a racist didn't hold water, because I had just received the City's Hero's Award for helping to solve the murder of an Asian man. Mayor Shaun Street had thanked me publicly for helping him win his second term in a tightly contested race. My community service to help people from diverse communities was documented. This Asian group just didn't expect for someone to counter their nonsense.

Though my show continued to climb in the ratings, it became increasingly frustrating to report to a program director who competed against those he managed. Colby had an afternoon show and would save artists for it under the pretense that they didn't want to do morning interviews. His rationale was that *Jonesy in the Morning* already got high ratings, so we should make sure the rest of the station shined as well.

As my contract approached expiration, Bruder said, "I would love to give you a ton of money in your renegotiations, but I can't do it with fourth place . . . third to first place, well, that gives me something to work with." The next week the ratings came out, and my show placed third, but Bruder never acknowledged that achievement or offered a congrats or gave me a salary increase.

"Is it true that you're pregnant?" Colby asked.

"Oh, yes, I am!" I replied with a big smile, along with my co-workers.

"Oh, no, hell, you're not! I went through that shit with Wendy. And I'll be damned if I'm going through it with you." You could hear the proverbial pin drop in the room. Everyone was stunned by Colby's attack.

When Wendy and Colby were at Power 99, he couldn't take being in the shadow of a woman. When she was on maternity leave, he thought that he would have his opportunity to shine. Instead, he exposed his own lackluster career.

Jonesy in the Morning continued to maintain its number-three rating. Even so, the more successful it was, the more problems Colby had with everything I did.

"Your gossip is too negative." Colby would often say, yet he'd insist that I do a gossip segment during his afternoon show to help him in the ratings. If Colby didn't see me at a station event, he would document that I wasn't there, when in fact I was. If I was occasionally late, then an issue was made of it, though I continued to deliver revenue and ratings.

Mary Catherine Sneed, chief operations officer for Radio One, heard the disgust in my voice over how Bruder and Colby were sabotaging my show. Sneed and I had met for dinner, and I informed her of everything I had witnessed and experienced. I thought that Sneed was an ally, but I was wrong.

Bruder and Colby intensified their efforts to sabotage me, and created a tense workplace by firing two members of my team, Sherry and Jay Black, without my knowledge. Then they refused to renegotiate with Bent Roc, so with all of my right-hand people gone, all that was left was me. As a result, the ratings went down from number three to number eight. I had committed the ultimate corporate sin; I had gone over the heads of my immediate managers and exposed them. And Bruder and Colby were used to being number twenty-five, so going back down to what they were used to did not frighten them in the least.

In addition, I was making five times their salary, growing more powerful in the community, and I was pregnant.

Though Bruder never renegotiated my contract, Catherine Sneed had sent an office e-mail that outlined my base salary and signing bonuses. We had come to terms. Then abruptly, Sneed stopped moving forward, because Colby reported to her that I still didn't participate in enough community events. Just that day, he had commended how despite being pregnant, I was still attending community events! Behind my back, he was asserting lies, which Catherine then forwarded to my attorney. Immediately I called to confront Colby: "Why would you lie and throw bullshit in my game? You know I'm trying to renegotiate my contract!"

Colby flipped. "What the fuck are you talking about? I'm tired of your shit!" It was obvious I had caught him off guard, and he was struggling to mount a defense. "If you wanna fucking quit, go ahead and quit!"

I laughed.

Colby denied sending the e-mails that my attorney and I were holding in our hands.

"Just quit, Jonesy. Why don't you just quit?"

My immediate telephone calls to Mary Catherine Sneed went unreturned. It was Memorial Day weekend.

Tuesday, May 31, 2005.

"I know that we've been negotiating back and forth, but the station has decided to end your contract," Steven Golsch said, in Bruder's office, at the end of my morning shift. "And we need you to sign this."

"I'm not signing anything." It was a release form, waiving my rights to sue, in exchange for $15,000.

"Do you have anything to say?"

"No, except I'm not signing anything. And I need to get my commercials on for Grown Folks Fridays." Bruder had never liked the Grown Folks Fridays because they were another income stream for me, and having them made me less dependent on the station. My commercials for Grown Folks Fridays were shut down. The Beat management also contacted Power 99 and threatened to sue if *they* aired the commercials.

General Manager *Lynn Bruder, Human Resources Manager Steven Golsch and COO Catherine Sneed were subsequently fired, after different intervals. Colby Colb is still at the station.*

THIRTEEN

KEPT IT MOVING

I smiled and kept it moving. I refused to be chased into a foxhole. I hadn't realized that I'd allowed walls to be built around my entire life. But I knew that I had to snap out of the funk I was in and honor myself and the precious baby in my womb.

Deidre was a friend who worked in sales. She advised me on damage control. "All right, get Kevin on the phone. You need to go on Wendy's show and not let The Beat have the last word, and just let niggas know."

"Whatever you need. Get here by two or three o'clock," Kevin said. Wendy hugged me when I walked in. She loved that I was going to stick it to Colby, because she hated him too. However, my intent was not to shit on The Beat but to empower my public self. And to tell the listeners that some radio stations try to undermine one's influence.

"**I** want to thank everyone for their support. But you'll soon know the truth behind my firing." By then, no one outside of my inner circle knew that I was pregnant. After the hour-long interview, Program Director Thea Mitchem phoned, offering her support and to discuss future possibilities.

Though I continued to put forth a brave face, I had unconsciously allowed Shaun to shut down my life. It had become work and home. That was my whole life. My dream home, which I had intended to be a safe haven and also an entertainment showcase, often sat silent. Newfound friends and Philly's elite never came to the parties I had imagined having.

"You don't know Philly like I know Philly. You don't want niggas knowing where you live. They'll set you up 'cause you talk too much shit on the radio," Shaun would often say. I lived like a paranoid recluse. Any man and most girlfriends were shut down because I didn't want Shaun to think I wasn't serious and committed to him.

The pregnancy was messy and complicated because of fibroids, which caused frequent visits to the hospital. Sometimes the pain would be so blinding that I would collapse to the floor. I was nauseous from sunup to sundown. Even plain old nothing made me vomit.

Tracy from Hot 97 coincidentally phoned me on the same day I had been fired. I was relieved that she hadn't heard the news, because that would have placed me in a vulnerable negotiating position for a new job. Assuming that I would be desperate, she would've offered me peanuts for a salary. On that call, she offered me an opportunity to fill in on the morning show for rapper Joe Budden for one week. The word was that Joe wanted to leave to finish recording his sophomore album, but Tracy didn't share that little tidbit, that she needed an experienced host. In spite of that, I knew Tracy was offering the opportunity of a lifetime: to return to HOT 97 permanently, with my own morning show. To the public, the radio station was saying that I was only a "fill in"—meanwhile, contracts were being negotiated behind the scenes for me to permanently helm the morning show. When one door closes, another opens. I was thrilled. The grace of God continued to protect me.

Feeling spooked by Colby's sentiments, I waited until Tracy made a financial offer before I told her I was pregnant. By then, news of my firing had spread like wildfire. Internet chat rooms and blogs wondered about my next move. Gossipmongers wanted to know the details of my firing. Other so-called inside sources, not knowing what had really occurred, just made up shit and passed it off as legitimate.

Tracy's salary offer was far less than what I required, so I continued the negotiations with Barry Mayo, the then general manager of Emmis Broadcasting. After completing one week on-air, I was offered the gig full time.

Miss Jones in the Morning on HOT 97.

Hallelujah! Amen.

When there was an official announcement, Ebro, the music director, and Barry Mayo knew the kind of hesitation that I felt, but went out of their way to make sure I knew that I was supported. Earlier in my radio career, Barry Mayo had appointed himself as my mentor because, as he'd said, "I believe in your talent." In every way these two gentlemen helped me give Emmis another chance.

Shaun, in a rare spiritual moment, said, "God is good. But make sure those niggas pay you."

Late in my pregnancy, and with fibroids, I was unable to endure the three hour and fifteen minute car ride each day. I inherited the previous morning-show staff of Tae, DJ Envy, Miss Info and Donnell Rawlings, who were my cohosts. From the beginning, I had a good relationship with Donnell Rawlings, but I thought he was more invested in his stand-up comedy career. DJ Envy, Tae and I formed an easy camaraderie, while I found Miss Info to be standoffish, and she had her own way of doing the gossip segment. Despite my early requests for her to limit the length of the segment to three to four minutes, she continued to drag it out to nine to ten minutes, which in radio is entirely too long. Instead of Miss Info accepting my direction, she would deflect my orders, which left me no other alternative than to require that I screen the information before she went on the air. Miss

Info was also ordered to stop text-messaging and e-mailing her friends during the show, as her actions created a distraction.

HOT 97 had a TV monitor and an ISDN line installed in my home so that I could broadcast from there. It was understood that, though my name was on the show, the producer was responsible for creating the content, and the cohosts were to support the producer's vision for each program. For example, Smack Fest, which was the brainchild of Miss Info, was a battle between two contestants to see who could smack each other the hardest in the face. The prize was Summer Jam concert tickets and a $1,000 cash prize. Sitting at home watching the stupid and desperate contestants, I thought the entire concept was ignorant. By the time I was physically in the New York City HOT 97 studios, the Smack Fest concept was over.

On July 4th, 2004, Charisse was married in a beautiful ceremony. Shaun had been on some bitch shit that morning, so I ended up attending the wedding alone. A woman sitting at the table noticed my big belly and asked if I had any names in mind. After shaking my head, the woman asked, "What do you think of the name Jalen?" Shaun later agreed that Jalen would be a solid name for our precious son.

By September, my house was being renovated to prepare for Jalen's arrival. Every time I saw Shaun, he had a hammer or some tool in his hand. He tore down walls and repaired the cabinets. He created an amazing nursery for Jalen, which was adorned with light blue carpeting, bright walls, a round cherrywood crib with a white-lace overhang and cherrywood Bellini furniture—armoire, changing table and rocking chair. Comedian Todd Lynn, who had joined the show, purchased a Bellini bassinette for us. My baby shower was fabulous. Thrown by Charisse, it looked like a wedding reception. It was held at the elegant Bianca's on the Park in Harlem. The color scheme was teal green and white. In Jalen's honor, Barry Mayo purchased a $1,000 cake with baby blocks spelling Jalen's name and trimmed in 24K gold. In attendance from HOT 97 management were about fifty people, my cohosts, Wendy Williams, Kevin Hunter, and LL Cool J's wife and her camp. Friends from Philly came, and New York listeners sent gifts. A stretch limousine was filled with gifts, complete with everything Jalen could use.

Because of my severe fibroids, Jalen Scott was born during a high-risk caesarean delivery in late December of 2004. The night before the birth, I decorated our Christmas tree from top to bottom. It was my wish that Jalen would come to a home decorated for Christmas. Shaun, his sister, Vania, and I arrived at the hospital at 5:00 A.M. Through the entire delivery, Shaun held my hand, as the doctors cut through my extensive fibroids to search for Jalen in my uterus. Shaun and I became frantic when hours passed before we could hold Jalen. Unbeknownst to us, Jalen had to have debris removed from his lungs. In the mere hours our precious baby had been in the world, he'd been through his own little drama. But when he was brought to us, Jalen was serene, with big brown eyes that stared at me. He was warm and perfect. It was a beautiful sight to see Shaun hold his son for the first time.

Though Shaun and I still had our problems, we were thrilled to establish a home for Jalen. For me, I was in love with our new baby and with my return to HOT 97. However, I still felt unloved and strangled. Shaun minimized outside access to me by friends and coworkers. "I don't want Ebro or anybody from work to have access to you after six o'clock. That should be family time." In my own home, I allowed Shaun to make me walk on eggshells. Coworkers sent e-mails to avoid causing a conflict.

One night shortly after I got pregnant, Shaun flipped when an old male friend phoned me at 3:00 A.M. I told my friend, "Look, my man doesn't want anybody calling me." Instead of believing that this friendship was platonic, and that my friend now understood that I was in a relationship, Shaun chose that opportunity to lose control.

"You keep telling me to work on the relationship, work on the relationship. A nigger calling at three o'clock in the morning, what type of shit is that?" he asked when our argument spiralled into the next morning, as his mother sat nearby, saying nothing.

I explained that he had to understand that sometimes shit happened that was completely out of my control. Old friends didn't know that I lived with a psycho. When people want to argue, they'll use any excuse to unleash their verbal assault.

"I'm tired of you reprimanding me. Tired of this bullshit!" I became so angry once that I punched a wall. Despite my responsibilities to Jalen and HOT 97, I can honestly say that my mind was never clear. I allowed myself to be unproductive and sidetracked by Shaun's control issues. I refused to take industry meetings after work. Here I was, at my professional height, helming a number-one morning show but because I was so stressed out from 5:00 A.M. to 10:00 P.M. with a growing baby and a moody man, all I could think of was avoiding a shitty argument and getting through my life without starting another one. Two entire years passed without maximizing any major career moves. At that point, I began seeing what my life would become if I did not become proactive.

And I am not that bitch.

I refuse to be that woman who sits home watching her baby when her man is out running the street every Friday, Saturday, and Sunday. And here I am, the breadwinner, paying all the bills, and I can't get anything? I can't go out? And when I do, it's a problem. Or when my friends call me, my man starts talking shit? Why is he listening to my phone conversations with my friends?

These were the thoughts that ran through my head.

Shaun began to tell me what I could and couldn't do professionally. That was when I finally woke up: "Who the hell are you to tell me what I can or cannot do professionally? You know what? I'm done, I don't want to be with you no more."

Shaun replied, "Are you serious?"

"Yes, I'm serious. I don't want you anymore. I'm done. There is no more love here. It's done. Get your shit and get out."

On December 26, 2004, I sat, holding Jalen, stunned as over 275,000 people lost their lives during an early-morning tsunami in Thailand, Indonesia, Africa and India. I was horrified. As a human being and a new mother, my heart went out to the frantic parents who were searching for their children.

It was my first day back after two weeks on maternity leave. My producer, Rick Delgado, formerly of the infamous *Opie & Anthony Show,* wrote and produced a parody, which I didn't hear in advance of its airing, satirizing disaster and relief efforts. Rick said that the parody was making fun of the celebrities that record music every time there's a catastrophe.

The Tsunami parody aired for three days straight without public outcry. There were minimal complaints from listeners, and none from coworkers or advertisers. In radio, there's an unwritten rule that team members express a united front. Any issues or disagreements should be addressed behind the scenes before anyone goes on the air, to prevent blindsiding of coworkers. On the third day the parody ran, Miss Info grandstanded on-air, separating herself from her coworkers in response to a boycott threat she had received from an Asian organization.

I accept responsibility for continuing to let the "Tsunami" song play for three days, and wasn't privy to any response to the station, as I continued to broadcast from home. From the beginning of the airing of the parody, I unwittingly followed the lead of Rick Delgado, my show's producer, as was station policy. However, that doesn't excuse my not deading the parody from the beginning. Blindsided was how I felt the morning Miss Info and I had our heated on-air exchange, which has become radio history.

TODD LYNN: Starring the Miss Jones in the Morning Players
MISS INFO: Minus Miss Info.
MISS JONES: Of course.
LYNN: Now, that's it damnit. Why is it all minus you? Why don't

you just quit if you don't want to be on the show? Why is it always you?

MISS INFO: That song is really offensive to me. And I opted to not involve myself.

JONES: Well, why do you always . . . if you feel that way . . . why are you on the show? You always have to separate yourself.

INFO: I support that all of you guys have the right to say anything that you want to and make fun of anything that you want to. And I understand that especially in a tragedy that is one way that people deal with it. But for me personally, I just felt that I needed to opt off of it because me personally I could not deal with it that way.

JONES: And while we all respected that . . . 'cause I don't think anybody was beating your door down for your vocals on the song . . . why do you have to always make it known that you are separate?

INFO: I-I—

JONES: You do! Even with celebrity drama, you always have to be like, "Well, I don't feel that way . . ." Well, it is not always a question if you agree or not . . . just give the damn gossip. . . . But I forget you are a journalist, right?

INFO: Everyone else gets to say their opinion—

JONES: It is not always about all of our opinions. But you always make like you separate. If you want to be separate, be separate. Go all of the way there—

INFO: You are misunderstanding.

JONES: Of course I am. But let's make it clear from here on out . . . you don't have to be a part of it—

INFO: No, I'm trying to—

JONES: No, you're not. You're not. You're always trying to undermine everything that is done here—

INFO: That is so ridiculous—

JONES: Okay, well, you guys have a nice day. And we appreciate you—we appreciate you riding with us.

DJ Envy: Can I say one thing?

Jones: What?

DJ Envy: *Miss Jones in the Morning* is brought to you by Sprint PCS—

Jones: "I don't feel that way"...."I was out of it"...—who cares? No one is asking ... you are always trying to put our asses out on the line further than yours.

Info: [Indecipherable]

Jones: Well you can't do it ... but that is what you are attempting.... This issue is bigger than the Tsunami song. It's bigger than the Tsunami song. Every time there is an artist ass to be kissed ... or an artist ass to be put out there, you opt for invitations to the parties.... You don't even do the job the way it is supposed to be done ... so you can have a different agenda.

Info: [Indecipherable]

Jones: I intend to ... I take it the way it is given.... I am not a damn fool and you probably think you are superior because you are Asian ... but you are not. You are not—

Info: That's ridiculous.

Jones: I know it is ridiculous the fact that you could be superior.

Info: I-I—

Jones: I-I ... Have a good day.

Info: Tomorrow morning when I ask how many stories are to be done in celebrity drama, please follow that. Thank you!

Jones: Sorry, Dr. Jeff, that you had to be here when family is fighting ... but it is what it is—

Info: Sometimes that's what I try to do—

Jones: No, it's not always necessary ... I tell you what, the next time, I am going to call you on the warm line.... Let's necessary that ... let's me and you deal like that.... Because if I had been there the microphones would have been off—

Info: Let's do it—

JONES: Have a great day . . . and I want you to have the same heart
that you are having now . . .
INFO: Okay.

Miss Info deserved an Academy Award for her victim portrayal. Never did she admit being notorious for calling Todd Lynn a "black gorilla" on and off the air. That night, Miss Info tried to contact me to apologize, but we kept playing phone tag, and never spoke. And haven't since. In our next team meeting, the cohosts confronted her with "You don't do that. You don't separate yourself from the team on-air." Afterward, everyone went home, not expecting the HOT 97 tsunami that was around the corner.

On January 17, 2005, the "Star & Buc Wild" show debuted on Clear Channel's Power 105.1. The show's return to the New York market was overshadowed by our "Tsunami" song situation, and Star took the opportunity to issue a quote to the *Daily News:* "That bitch is a wrap."

Three days later, Barry Mayo called me at home. "We have a problem. The city is in an uproar and your head is on fire."

"That's bullshit. I never had control over my show."

"We need to talk." Barry drove to my home in Philly.

To this day, I don't know, nor do I want to know, what level of management maintained the task of approving the content of *Miss Jones in the Morning.* The only thing I do know is that everything had to be preapproved before the broadcast. And I was rarely consulted. The bottom line is that I neither created nor added content to nor sang on the "Tsunami" song. I have been accused of having all levels of involvement, and that is wrong.

I was guilty of not deading a song that I knew wasn't funny. But because Rick was the producer, I trusted and followed his direction. When my teammates and I would come up short on comedy or social-awareness content, Rick was there giving an angle to take.

Soon after my on-air "conversation" with Miss Info, Emmis lawyers conducted their own investigation, interviewing everyone.

Sitting in my living room that afternoon with Barry and Shaun, who had returned from spending the afternoon in the park with Jalen, I felt helpless, and Barry was nervous. "Your job is on the line."

"You let her go, you're gonna have so much pressure from advertisers that you'll need to bring her back." Shaun read the situation tight. Everyone was running scared and I was the sacrificial lamb.

"You don't know what you're talking about. I've been honest with her from the beginning."

"Bullshit! You're trying to set her up," Shaun countered.

Barry looked at Shaun and then at me. "Are you going to trust him or are you going to trust me?"

As he left the house, Barry advised me to take some paid days off. To the *Daily News,* he said, "There is no timetable for deciding what happens from here."

The HOT 97 website posted the following:

OFFICIAL STATEMENT ON AIRING

OF TSUNAMI PARODY SONG

January 21, 2005

HOT 97 regrets the airing of material that made light of a serious and tragic event. We apologize to our listeners and anyone who was offended.

HOT 97 takes pride in its community involvement and in the last few weeks has joined with broadcasters nationwide to raise money for victims of the Tsunami. Our relief effort will result in a substantial cash donation.

As an additional sign of HOT 97's commitment to the cause, Miss Jones in the Morning, along with her entire staff, have agreed to contribute one week's pay to Tsunami Relief efforts.

Taking my life into my own hands, I sought counsel from my sister Audrey, who contacted Nancy Grace, an old colleague from Court TV.

The feedback was that I'd probably have a successful lawsuit if I was fired, but I needed to know if that was what I really wanted.

I loved working at Emmis Communications, but more importantly, I wanted to clear my name. The trust factor amongst the team members was gone. No one trusted anyone, primarily because Rick didn't step forward and take responsibility for creating the song. He had to be smoked out; he had stood by and let the media slaughter me.

During my three-week suspension, I was depressed. The situation was fucked up, because it seemed that the "Tsunami" thing would always be a part of who I was, and there was this child that I had brought into the world, and people were going to judge him based on what his mother was alleged to have done. I couldn't take it. I refused communication with the outside world.

High-profile attorney Mel Sachs was retained as my counsel and he advised me to be quiet and let him do the talking. Mel arranged for me to meet with Queens Council Member John Liu at City Hall. I felt that Liu had his mind made up about the situation before he met me and was focused on getting reelected.

"It's over, Jonesy. It's over," an understandably depressed Todd Lynn phoned to say.

"It's really an unfortunate thing, Todd. But thank God you're talented. I know you'll get another gig." In an interview with hiphopmusic.com, Todd was quoted as saying: "What I will tell you is Miss Jones had nothing to do with the writing or producing of the song or the voicing. She works from home and has been doing that for several months."

Naysayers have often drawn comparisons to my reactions to Star during the Aaliyah incident with that of the "Tsunami" parody. "Jonesy was up on her high horse with Star, now she's acting like she can't relate to what Miss Info did."

To me, these are two entirely different situations.

The important difference is that before the show, I asked Star not to air the plane-crash sound effects. Further, I informed him what the consequences would be if he did. When he aired the sound effects, Star wasn't shocked by my reaction. He had been put on notice. He knew that I would follow through with my warning. Further, I didn't grandstand and separate myself from the team once the microphones were on. Miss Info, however, did. She waited for the microphones to go on to make her position known, which means she wasn't sincere. She let the parody air for three mornings before she said anything about it. And Miss Info had waited until she was contacted by an Asian organization and informed that they were about to come after us. From that point, she heard the protests and decided to protect her own self-interest by any means necessary. If that meant sacrificing the careers of anyone else on the show, then so be it.

6:46 A.M. February 14, 2005

"I need a moment. First of all, I want to say that I am very happy to be back, and grateful for the chance to be back. And I want to, once again, apologize from the bottom of my heart for offending y'all, and especially the families of the victims of the tsunami. We are so sorry. Although I didn't write or sing on the 'Tsunami' song . . . some people think that was me on it . . . it was in very bad poor taste, and we all showed poor judgment in airing it. It was a bad thing to do, and we hope you can forgive us. Once again, thank you for the chance for being back here."

Still broadcasting from home, I felt like my show had disintegrated into tiny little pieces. Todd was gone. Rick was gone. Envy, Tae, and I were left, strong but feeling a little wounded. For the most part, the listeners were very supportive. Even the ones who condemned the parody admitted that we are all human and can inadvertently act without judgment.

DJs from other parts of the day, such as Angie Martinez and Funkmaster Flex, extended themselves beyond the call of duty by offering to do free appearances and gigs for any of the advertisers. For the first time, I felt that the entire HOT 97 staff was, and is, family.

Unfortunately, Star and Wendy Williams used their coveted broadcasts to attack me during the "Tsunami" situation, in a manner that has never been seen before in New York radio. So much for there being a fraternal network of broadcasters. Black unity. Supporting one another. Those are all slogans that look great on T-shirts.

"Her son is a mongoloid with Down syndrome," Star snarled to his listeners on countless mornings. "Oh, yeah, I effed that bitch in the back of her Mercedes-Benz." When he debuted at Clear Channel's Power 105.1 in January of 2005, he used four hours of drive time—high-end broadcast real estate—to slander my name to millions. And for months, I didn't respond.

"Yeah, her son is a mongoloid . . . I'll pay five hundred bucks to anyone who will get her son's medical records and send them to me at the station. You get the medical records, and I'll pay $500. Somebody help me. No man in his right mind is going to marry her. Miss Jones is a whore. That's why she has a baby and no husband," Star continued.

During the spring of 2006, Star added DJ Envy to his focus and produced promotional spots offering money to whomever could find where DJ Envy's children attended school. The following are words that the advocate of hate, Troi "Star" Torain, spoke on the air:

"Somebody holla at me and tell me about his whore wife and his kid: 866-678-8270. Somebody get at me about his whore. His whore wife and his kid, this little ugly-ass kid, I hear. Where, where does this kid go to school? I got five hundred bucks for that information. Somebody e-mail or gimme a call. Just tell me where his kid goes to school. Let's see who's really gully on the microphone. Five hundred dollars, in my pocket, right now. I need to know the school this faggot-ass nigga DJ's kid goes to school."

What happened to the love Star professed for me when he had me fired from the morning show that we had cohosted? Were those crocodile tears that he'd shed? "I love you, Miss Jones. Don't forget that." Were those constant telephone calls to my friend Charisse to see how I was doing a giant ruse? Damn. His type of love must be a fleeting thing.

Star has a habit of planning a vendetta against every station that's fired him. From MTV and HOT 97 to Power 105.1. He's remained bitter against the record labels that never hired him. In every situation, Star has created chaos, even when there were opportunities for his return. When he broke all of the framed photos hanging in the hallways of HOT 97 and stood toe-to-toe with the then-general manager Barry Mayo, there'd still been a chance that he could be brought back. Yet he blew it.

Now his vendetta had shifted to target not only corporations, but also innocent children. Never in his warped fantasy of the world did he think that the previously thin-skinned Miss Jones would rise to be recognized for her true value and successfully compete with the big boys of broadcasting. For Star, I was just an easy mark. Never before in corporate warfare has a strategy been so calculating, and so inept.

With me on the air at HOT 97, Star sensed that "Miss Jones in the Morning" would be a serious challenge. It should have come as no surprise to him that evidence of my value had been building. Exploding.

For Star, it must be painful to twice have been on the top of New York radio, the number-one market in the country, and to have overplayed his hand, squandering millions of dollars. I only ask, was it worth it? Paraphrasing the words of Rodney King, couldn't we have all just gotten along?

Ever since I pulled a weekend shift at HOT 97, Wendy Williams has attacked me whenever the mood struck her. "Jonesy Clonesy" and "There is just one queen of radio" are some of the insults that Wendy would take time out of her life to hurl my way. My mistake was not shutting her down sooner. She and her husband thought it was hilarious to perform unanswered monologues about me to titillate her listeners. Her insecure ass was focused on me, though I am younger and contracted on a completely different radio station and in an opposite time slot. Actually, it's a compliment that I consume her thoughts to that extent. But it seems like she'd have better things to do. Still, at her age, Wendy admits that she is very insecure and has low self-esteem. In her position, she should be professionally riding the wave as leader of the pack or sharing the torch gracefully, knowing she will get love from young ones like myself who desire mentorship. Wendy wants to not only hold on to the torch, but also crush anyone who dares to have aspirations for success. Her justification has always been: "I'm not helping nobody, because nobody helped me." In hindsight, I realize Wendy didn't refer me to the Philadelphia radio station out of generosity. Like Star, she underestimated me—she never thought I would join her as being one of the few black women hosting their own radio show in a top market.

Her husband, Kevin Hunter, told me when he first met Wendy that his intention was to ride her gravy train. And nothing has changed. Wendy needed someone to fight her battles, in case people objected to the things she said. And Kevin pretends that he's her selfless crusader.

It's a shame that Star and Wendy wanted me dead in radio. But God be the glory, I'm still here. Evil doesn't always prevail. I continue to evolve as a mother, a broadcaster, a human being. I've learned to identify my own strengths and weaknesses. And my goals are no longer measured by the standard of success established by others. It only matters what will in the long run create value in my life, and in the life of my beautiful son.

FOURTEEN

JONESY'S ZONE

Celebrities and notables, people on their way up and on their way out have appeared on *Miss Jones in the Morning*. Depending on the day and guest, controversy has been created, good times have been had, mischief promoted, and empowering information delivered, resulting in compelling, top-rated programming. Compelling in the sense that celebrities and their lackey publicists are on notice that I, together with my program director and cohosts, guide the direction of the interview. My responsibility is to deliver to the two-million-plus listeners original content, as opposed to boring, cookie-cutter responses that can be copied and pasted from any show. And if a celebrity guest comes with another agenda, I'll be more than happy to let them know that this is *my* house.

My cohosts and I don't plot to ambush any guest, but what gets me heated is when someone who's getting free promotion for their product or service decides to shut down, to not answer any questions. The listeners are thinking, "Well what is so-and-so there for?" Extensive research is conducted on every issue, on every rumor and on every guest who appeals to our audience. Like court attorneys, we already know the answers to our questions, before they're even posed. My listeners despise insincerity and game-playing. Their sentiment is: "Oh! So you want me to buy your CD, but you won't tell me why you and dummy broke up?"

That's a no-go at *Miss Jones in the Morning.* When a celeb enters our studio, they've crossed into the bullshit-free zone. Celebrities need to decide, in Tina Turner's immortal words, "Nice and easy or nice and rough." When guests sit before our microphones, they have a duty to be responsive and lively, informative and willing to expose a little bit of their vulnerability. Celebrities who only want to promote a stupid CD or a lame movie that's headed straight to video need not apply. To ignore the beat of the streets and floating rumors, while so-and-so drones on about their soon-to-be-canceled television show, is being dishonest. My microphone allows for give-and-take, not just a boring monologue from a celeb who wants my listeners to buy their shit. Sorry. Wrong show.

I'll continue to provide information and perspectives that my devoted listeners will respond to. Otherwise, they'll begin to fill their radio appetite elsewhere.

I am forever mindful that in radio, content is king, and my listeners deserve more.

Sean "P Diddy" Combs: The first time I interviewed Diddy, he threatened to put me in the trunk of a car. I'd been constantly making sarcastic comments about his first album, *No Way Out.* I had no respect for him as an artist. There was really no love between us. I thought he was riding the coattails of Biggie Smalls and made no secret of it, by saying so. But I didn't hate him. Later, when we requested an interview, Diddy called my private cell number to ask if I was going to ambush him. He said, "What kinda questions are you going to ask?"

It was kind of ironic to have Diddy, who was building careers for others and an empire for himself, asking me to take it easy on him. I respected that a man of his stature would be humble enough to make that gesture. Diddy still kept me at arm's length, knowing how relentless I can be on the microphone. Some celebrities can't separate my views on their art from my view of them personally. Two separate issues. When Diddy was arrested for weapons charges, I relentlessly discussed his romance with singer/actress Jennifer Lopez, whether she would dump him or not; if Diddy really bribed his chauffeur; rapper Jamal "Shyne" Barrow's involvement. When the trial date was set, I laid it on so thick that he called and begged me to stop talking about it.

"This is my life," Diddy said quietly.

Diddy's humility was impressive, so I respected his wishes and backed off. Things were cool between us, but we were not huggy-huggy. That was fine.

Remembering what I did, Diddy granted me the first interview after his acquittal. A few years later I saw him at Summer Jam and he hollered from his VIP booth, "Hey! Wassup, Miss Jones?!" Diddy and I hugged and caught up on each other's lives. His hit MTV television show, *Making the Band 2,* had debuted and Diddy decided to incorporate my media-training company with the show. My assignment was to torment members of Da Band to help them build some muscle for handling the media. Our related careers have grown together side by side. Diddy now considers me to be a fellow OG. He knows that even though I respect him immensely, I won't hesitate to "bring it" if a headline warrants.

Mary J. Blige: My interview with Mary went so well. I understood her life story. She shared the details on her relationship with ex-boyfriend KC and how they used to do drugs. But that's where the commonality ends, because I'm just not feeling her music. I respect her business vision, but her music and live performances are just too inconsistent. Perhaps the tone of her albums and their release dates

didn't coincide with what was going on in my life. When she was experiencing her depressed stage and expressing it in the *My Life* album, I wasn't feeling all of that. There was a dark cloud over her. She was depressed and I wasn't. I couldn't join her legion of fans in holding lit candles in the air. Color me evil, but I'm not there yet.

Whenever Mary made headlines I would comment in whatever flippant manner I was working with at the moment. "Bring back drunk and druggy Mary. 'Cause I'm not feeling all of this kumbaya crap," I would say. I soon learned that she is one of those artists who doesn't want to be asked compelling questions or to be joked about. For a public figure, she has thin skin. I would joke about her midget husband's funny-sounding name. It was a joke. No evil intent. Just fun albeit at Mary's expense.

"Why is your girl talking about my wife?" her husband, Kendu Isaacs, asked when he phoned Ebro to complain, thinking that he could control my mouth. Ebro would never order me to stop joking about any public figure.

In August 2006 at HOT 97's Summer Jam, Mary went onstage and shouted out the names of station DJs Angie Martinez, Fat Man Scoop, Flex, and Mister Cee. The next morning during our report on the concert, I called Mary a bitch for coming to my house, the place that I work, and deliberately trying to isolate me from my coworkers. The *New York Daily News* reported that I had past issues with Mary, which is not the case. I have never had any personal dealing with Mary J. Blige.

Her omission was not what I found insulting. It was the mere fact that she had made a point out of it by coming to my house and taking a stab at me. Mary fell and broke her ass onstage in front of thousands afterward. Karma is a bitch.

Christina Milian: Christina contacted the show wanting to be interviewed. We didn't call her. She contacted us on the heels of being dropped by Def Jam and her public hookup and breakup with Nick Cannon. After pleasantries were exchanged, it was clear that Christina had another agenda—to promote her new movie, *Pulse*. Instead of letting me toot her horn and encourage my listeners to go see the flick, Christina announced what she was and was not there to talk about.

Wrong move.

Since Christina had been quoted extensively in other media about her relationships with Def Jam and Nick Cannon, my listeners deserved to be updated on what had happened between them.

"How you guys doing?" Christina asked.

"We're fine. How are you?"

"I'm doing good. I'm in LA, so you know it's early."

"Oh, wow! Well, we appreciate you getting up so early to talk to us."

"Oh, it's no problem. Thank you guys for taking time out today."

"We were a little concerned. We heard you left Def Jam. We heard it was because your mom was overly involved in your career and Def Jam didn't appreciate it."

"Um, that's not the truth." Christina pretends to laugh.

"That's why we're glad you called."

"Huh?"

"I said, that's why we're glad you called. So then, what was the reason?"

"It had nothing to do with that. It had nothing to do with any of the rumors put out there. The label and I weren't happy with each other and the result was dipping record sales. So you know, it was time to move on."

"Did it have anything to do with you not selling any records, Christine?" Michael Shawn piped in.

"Huh?"

"Did it have anything to do with you not selling any records?" he repeated.

"Well, you never know. It had to do with a lot of different things, so— We were both unhappy and at the end of the day. We made history with Def Jam and it's time for a new start."

"Right. But before we can get to the start, we got to. . . . What were you unhappy with Def Jam about?" I asked.

"Um, the reason I have not spoke on it is for a reason. And it's business. And I'm very careful with my business."

"Oh, she suing," I say.

"At the end of the day—"

"She suing," I repeat.

While Christina is talking but not making sense, I blurted, "Who's handling the case?"

"What did you say?" Christina asked.

"Who's handling the lawsuit?"

"That's all on the attorneys."

"Nice. Nice, Christina. Nice Jonesy that you read that," Michael Shawn said.

"Did you turn down Rihanna's song? Did L.A. Reid say to do Rihanna's song and you didn't want to do it?" DJ Envy asked.

"That has nothing to do with—"

"No, he's just asking the question."

"Just asking did you turn down Rihanna's song."

"Huh?"

"Did you turn down Rihanna's song? That smash single. Did you turn that down?" DJ Envy asked for a fourth time.

"That has nothing to do with this movie that's coming out right now."

"Christina, can you just answer the question? Yes or no. Did you turn down the song?" Though I sounded composed, by now I was losing patience. She hadn't answered one question and we were running out of time.

"You know, I-I-I am honestly here to talk about the movie and I'm not talking about any of that stuff. And I have to be very careful."

"Oh, okay. The conversation is over. Thank you," I said.

Click.

I hung up the telephone and spoke to the listeners. "You can't come on this show and think you're going to dictate the direction of the interview."

It's too early in the morning for all of that bullshit. She knew where she was calling and the concept and tone of the show. Christina thought she was going to get an Angie Martinez type of interview— nice and soft. And though I respect Angie, nice and soft is not how the on-air character of Miss Jones is defined. If Christina's relationship with Def Jam or Nick Cannon had been secret all along, perhaps there would have been some leeway. And no one wanted to hear about her bullshit movie.

She didn't want to talk about why she got dropped by Def Jam. She didn't want to talk about if she was suing them. She didn't want to talk about her and Nick Cannon. And I'm like, "Get the fuck outta here. Nothing else interests us."

She wanted to control the interview, and that will never happen.

Beyoncé Knowles: Beyoncé's singing, writing, and dancing talent is absolutely awesome, but her acting leaves something to be desired. When I interviewed her, she was still with Destiny's Child and they were still hillbilly bitches.

Not too long ago, when she was scheduled to be interviewed at HOT 97's sister station, KISS-FM, we passed in the hallway between studios and she moved in to hug hello. Since I don't do the whole hugging thing, I kept her at bay, which is my prerogative. Seeing this exchange, her mother, Tina Knowles, approached me. Instead of being happy that her daughter and I spoke, the coattail-riding mother said, "Thank you for talking about Beyoncé so much. It really keeps her ratings up," and walked away, followed by a shocked entourage.

"And bitch, I will continue to keep talking about her, and you!" I yelled after her.

Fuck Tina Knowles and her barrel-assed hip daughter and her stepdaughter Kelly! If she only had that much heart when it came to her philandering husband, perhaps she wouldn't come off like a hypocrite.

Tina's face had cracked because she didn't know what to say, and she just kept walking. But I continued, getting louder, "As a matter of fact, I'm gonna talk about your ass tomorrow!"

Unbeknownst to the listeners, the amelobastoma, the tumor that I was first treated for in high school, had returned. But this time my condition required hospitalization, surgery, and three weeks of rehabilitation. The morning face-off with Tina was my last day on-air before the surgery. Before the anesthesia could wear off, the lies had spread that Tina Knowles had complained to the program director and that I had been suspended for three weeks. Nothing could have been further from the truth. Tina Knowles doesn't have that kind of power.

DJ Envy and Michael Shawn created a funny bit to instigate some controversy and exaggerated what actually occurred. Envy joked that I had said to Tina, "Actually, you should thank M.A.C. makeup for hiding all that oldness you have on your face. Now you look like the joker."

After the anesthesia wore off, as I lay in the hospital bed and heard about the rumor mill, I shook my head in disbelief. "Some people will believe anything!"

The Internet blogs and gossip hounds fell for it, hook, line and sinker. Loyal listeners called the radio station to demand that the fake suspension be lifted. Some people licked their lips over my possible demise, to the point where Assistant Program Director Ebro had to go on the air and explain that it had been a big hoax. But people still believed what they wanted to believe, until I returned to the airwaves and clarified that I'd had jaw surgery to remove the tumor.

Monica: The singer Monica asked to appear on the show to promote her new single, "Everytime tha Beat Drop." Monica confirmed the interview, but was then a no-show. Which is something you don't do if you're trying to promote your music in the New York market. When she didn't appear, I went on to discuss her new song. Frankly, I hate that effin' song, because it doesn't represent Monica's talent in a good light. Her fans and I know her to be the singer who sang Brandy under the rug on the duet "The Boy Is Mine." And that was my props to Monica.

It is my opinion that Monica had chosen not to sing on her new song and was trying to sound like Ciara. That's what I said. And that's how I felt. It seemed that Monica was dumbing down her talent to appease youngin' by releasing non-singing stuff. Stuff like "Chicken

Noodle Soup," which HOT 97 plays and kids love. But the real singing and artistry is not appreciated, so Monica must be trying to appeal to the youngin'.

Niggas always wanna encourage some beef, so that couldn't be the end of my critique, one morning DJ simply voicing her opinion about the music. Word got back. I don't know what the word was, but Monica met up with Power 105.1's DJ Clue, who hasn't had a clue since he left HOT 97. Monica was alleged to have said, "Miss Jones is on this shit but when I saw Jonesy it was all hugs and kisses."

I haven't laid eyes on Monica Norton since 2003. If she'd seen me, it probably *would* have been hugs and kisses, but I haven't seen her!

DJ Clue, seeing an opportunity to stir up some shit, replied, "I see Monica wants to get it poppin'!"

Later, during an interview on V-103's Frank Ski and Wanda, an Atlanta station, Monica brought up what I said. "Y'all ever hear of Miss Jones? She was, like, roasting me. It was funny to me because it's been a big thing about me singing over the snap music, which I didn't think there should be. I always try to have my game face on, use my good voice and be grammatically correct and everything, but Miss Jones really took me there. I thought I'd left those days behind. I heard this thing where she was saying that 'Everytime tha Beat Drop' was an awful song. And that I had no business singing it, and why would I dumb down my vocals like girls like Ciara? I was offended immediately, because you're talking about girls from Atlanta. I don't play games with Ciara. She may not defend herself, but I defend her. Then Miss Jones was saying that I was weird-looking and skinny. I was shocked. Shocked. You know how I am. I treat everyone the same, and it will never change. And the next thing I know, she calls me the B word."

V-103 cohost Wanda said, "Girl, call Air Tran! We're going to New York!"

Monica replied, "We can't take what I'm bringing! We'll go to jail after we finish."

My comments were never personal to Monica. They were backhanded compliments. No insults were made about her. That being said, I, as a person and as a morning-show host, have the right to not like a song when I don't like it. I never said that I don't like Monica and she can't sing. When I know that Monica is on a record, I want to hear her sing. Gimme what I want. Now she's turning the situation into something else. Everything that she's said in interviews with the Atlanta radio station and Eurweb.com, she should've simply said to me. And focused on promoting Monica.

The biggest misconception about me is that I'm ruled by my ego. That is a false impression, because I rise at 3:30 A.M. each morning to expose myself, right or wrong, to millions. While I'm not afraid to express a wide range of emotions before virtual strangers, off-air my life experiences have helped me to mature and become more introspective. Instead of fighting worthless battles, I now question my intent and seek solutions regarding any given situation. Sometimes the answers come through when I choose to become quiet. In other instances, I welcome the opportunity to learn whatever life sends my way. And during still other times, I may be inclined to say, "Fuck it."

The beauty has been in knowing that there's strength in asking for support. And even though I experienced early disappointments from those who loved me or claimed to, I no longer want to go through my life fighting, on the defense, as I once did.

I have relinquished carrying the burden of my mother's life, and the lives of all of my departed loved ones. I have learned that I can't avenge their dreams and survive to live my own life. It's exciting to start anew and explore a more healing direction. My dear mother, Alyce, had her own issues, which caused her to make the decisions she made. And I took notes as a child, trying to wear her behaviors in my life. But they didn't fit. My stepfather, father, and sisters have lived with the tools they were given. There is no denying that with every breath, they have labored to do better, in spite of their personal challenges. Even through their aloofness and criticism, they've still expressed undying love for me. And I am forever grateful.

Now instead of looking at them with a critical eye, pointing a finger, I'm determined to focus on myself. Only then can there be true change for me. Now I know that I have no power to change others, nor is it my responsibility. My family relationships have shown the impact that I can have on others. I accept the fact that I'm far from perfect. But there's a beauty in imperfection, and I look forward to my own evolution.

The woman millions hear each morning is a combination of several different personas that I created. The distinction is that you'll find the characteristics of my on-air persona in Tarsha, but you won't find Tarsha in those characteristics. When I sound unconquerable and unflinching behind the microphone, there's still a concerned, soft and cuddly woman who enjoys a game of double Dutch with her longtime friends. When I'm screaming on the biggest movie star, there's still a chick who goes home and plays peekaboo with her wonderful baby.

I remain conflicted by a society that often delivers bullshit but then criticizes me for rejecting it; a world that instigates a fight and then takes me to task when I swing; an entertainment industry that creates false images and hates me for looking behind the facade and drawing my own conclusions.

My life, with all of its struggle and grace, continues to be blessed. I pray every day in appreciation, as all I have accomplished is beyond my wildest dreams. At one time, attending the High School of Music & Art and Syracuse University was only a dream. Moving from singing into a hairbrush to performing on national stages was a dream that I wanted but never thought I would come close to experiencing. I'm grateful that I allowed God to work in mysterious ways, so that I wasn't limited to the dream I thought I wanted, not knowing that a far bigger and fulfilling stage awaited—my career in radio.

Despite my struggles with romantic relationships, I will never give up on embracing true love from a compassionate and loving man.

There's a lot more coochie-popping left in this woman. But now I'm willing to wait for the man to take the lead and show me who he is, as opposed to me dancing as fast as I can to prove my worthiness.

It continues to be a lifelong struggle, and I wish it would stop hurting to be accused of something I haven't said or done. But it hasn't. I do enough fucked-up shit that I'm more than willing to take the fall for. I just don't need extra shit thrown in the game. I've learned to restrain myself from always reacting; now I pick my battles. And I hope that my fans, family, and friends will continue to support me, because there are many miles to go before I sleep. I remain packed for the lifelong journey.

I appreciate you taking the time to read my story. Instead of jumping on a bandwagon, forming a hysterical opinion and a perception about who I am from a two-second sound bite, I hope that listeners will know that there's more to me than what they hear from 6:00 A.M. to 10:00 A.M. each morning. When the next controversy occurs with my name attached, I hope that instead of running with half-truths based upon someone's desire for my downfall, you'll consider these pages and challenge my detractors by asking, *Have You Met Miss Jones?*

WITH DEEP APPRECIATION

I have never felt more loyalty, or known that it existed, than when I met DJ Envy, Tasha Hightower, Shawnee Culture, Michael Shawn, and Ebro. I never knew that loyalty amongst coworkers could run so deep. But in each of them I've found a piece of life that I was missing. Their friendship has been what I need every day to perform like a well-oiled machine. Each one of my teammates is like organs vital to my radio being, and without them I couldn't produce.

DJ Envy: His strength is so subtle and unending. I always know what to expect from him. When I need huge favors, Envy is the bank that I trust. By being calculating and mature, DJ Envy got rid of Star and beat him at his own game. Envy stood up on the air and called Star a coward. Envy's courageous defense of my son was the spark that lit the flame that caused Star to shift attention from me to Envy. Envy portrayed the strength of manhood as Star unleashed a fury of insults on his family. "His wife had trains run on her at Hampton. She ain't nothing but a gook. Ha! Ha!" Star said. To DJ Envy, courageous men are always victorious.

Michael Shawn: I thank him for believing in me and joining me in the mornings when we were in the thickness of battle and daggers were coming from everyplace we could imagine. And while I know there has been a paycheck involved, I see how little that means since he consistently shows his devotion. Thank you to Michael for being a soldier.

Ebro: Congratulations on your appointment to HOT 97 Program Director!! All of your hard work has paid off. This man has helped me to not get caught up in emotion and to remain focused. I thank him for not being afraid when I yelled and pushed him far away. I meant better, but couldn't see beyond my own insecurities. I thank him for being unbiased when I'm out of line and about to destroy everything, and for reminding me how far and how hard I've worked. And how to keep it all in perspective, with the same passion today as I had when I first returned to New York City's HOT 97.

Tasha Hightower: Tasha is a real girlfriend. I doubted her at first, but through time she has proven her loyalty. She is such a talented, brilliant, hardworking young woman, who has overcome odds, especially being a single mother. I thank her for dabbing my tears and holding me up and reminding me how much I deserve to be happy, so that I could focus on helping other people laugh in the morning. I know she doesn't get the credit she deserves, but I will never forget her. She will always shine brightly and be taken care of.

Shawnee Culture: Shawnee understands my hormonal imbalance and is always right where I need him to be—on my right-hand side. He makes me sound better. His brilliance in reading my thoughts and anticipating the next moment is even better than my former boyfriends. Shawnee is the best.

Barry Mayo: Barry has been a powerful mentor and friend. I appreciate how he reminds my sisters and me how much we need one another, and leads by example. He is honorable, incredibly brilliant, strategic, and a motivating force in my life. Thank you, Barry, for convincing me of that and promising to bring me back to New York.

My sisters, Audrey and Marcia: Who would have thought that those three little girls who lived in 5G in the Astoria Projects would have accomplished so much? Personally and professionally, I admire your victories, resiliency, your brilliance and vulnerability. I am honored that you are my sisters. You both have set the standard for achievement in me, your little sister. Even during life's challenges, I love you both for always keeping the light on.

My dear son, Jalen: You are perfection. Every day I marvel at your blossoming unique personality. You are precious and lovable. You have such a bright light inside with such a brilliance in your curiosity about the world. You are sweet, strong, kind, and cuddly. You will become a great man, accomplishing great things.

Jacqui Powell: My lifetime friend and navigator. You have been the purest definition of a friend. Selfless. Kind. Always encouraging. I love the secrets we share. Please know that I recognize that because of my demanding schedule, you may have been a greater friend to me than I have been to you. I will always love your lion heart.

Sabrina: Thank you for showing my words how to dance and for protecting my story by reminding me every step of the way how important it was that it be told. Without your eloquence and unwavering support this book couldn't have happened.

Melody: Thank you for believing in me. Thank you for being interested in my story. You have been a blessing in my life and definitely what the doctor ordered for my healing.

To K: Your love and encouragement transformed me and now the world will see what you and I already know. I love you and admire your strength. I look forward to spending the rest of our lives together.

INDEX

ABOUT THE AUTHORS

TARSHA JONES is the host of the Arbitron number-one-rated New York Hot 97 weekday morning show, "Miss Jones in the Morning." She attended New York City's Fiorello H. La Guardia High School of Music & Art and Performing Arts, as well as Syracuse University, where she graduated with a B.A. in music. She has recorded with Common, Jaheim, AZ, Big Pun, and the jazz artist Najee. Miss Jones lives in the New York area with her son.

The collaborator, SABRINA LAMB is a frequent on-air media commentator in New York City. She is the author of *Keepin' It Real: The Rise of Bullshit in the Black Community* [2007, Cambridge House Books] and *Have You Met Miss Jones?* [2007, Random House]. She is also the Chief Flirting Officer of FlirtingTime.com. A former stand-up comic, Lamb has appeared on Lifetime Television's *Girl's Night Out* and NBC's *Saturday Night Live*. Most notably, Lamb is the Founder/Executive Director of WorldofMoney.org, dedicated to the financial literacy of underserved youth.

ABOUT THE TYPE

This book was set in Granjon, a modern recutting of a typeface produced under the direction of George W. Jones, who based Granjon's design upon the letter forms of Claude Garamond (1480–1561). The name was given to the typeface as a tribute to the typographic designer Robert Granjon.